BLESSED

Rudolf Steiner
on
The Beatitudes

Adrian Anderson PhD

**Contemplating the Beatitudes from the
ancient Greek of St. Matthew's Gospel**

Threshold Publishing, Australia, 2018
www.rudolfsteinerstudies.com

Distributed by Ebooks Alchemy P/L
Windsor VIC 3181
Australia

ISBN 978-0-648135838

Contents

Introduction   1

Chapter One   13
The context of the commentaries from Rudolf
Steiner

Chapter Two   22
Rudolf Steiner's commentaries on Beatitudes 1, 2, 3

Chapter Three   42
Rudolf Steiner's commentaries on Beatitudes 4, 5, 6

Chapter Four   55
Rudolf Steiner's commentaries on Beatitudes 7, 8, 9

Chapter Five   64
Archive lecture of August 1904 (extract)

Chapter Six   68
Archive lecture of June 1905

Chapter Seven   94
Further Insights into the Beatitudes

Conclusion   115

Appendices
1: The soul-body as separate from the sentient-soul   116
2: The Essenes and the 'poor in spirit'   118
3: Last section of the 1905 lecture   120
4: "You are Gods"   126
5: The First Beatitude and the power of Christ   127

Index   130

Other books by the author
Website

"The words of Jesus are the Treasuries of Wisdom which proclaim through these teachings, from 'the Blessings' (*Beatitudes*), what is of primary importance and relevance to oneself."

Origenes   (in Alexandria, about AD 220)

Introduction

The Beatitudes are teachings of Christ, in the Gospel of St. Matthew, which begin with the words, "Blessed are...". They are proclamations about a blessed future condition beckoning to humanity. Together with the Lord's Prayer, the Beatitudes are regarded as the most sublime spiritual teachings in the New Testament.

The future of our planet is now under question, both through ecological damage, the dehumanizing of human beings through unwise engagement with technology, and also the potential for huge wars. Hence teachings oriented towards the future, suggesting any positive outcome, can easily be regarded by people today as naïve or as no longer relevant.

But such pessimism is not necessarily a true weather vane; for we human beings cannot accurately predict what the future may bring. That times of evil and wars would be a part of the 'karma' of our planet on into the future was surely well-known to Christ. Since his Beatitudes imply a successful outcome is possible for humanity in general, this suggests that a positive view of the future remains reasonable.

Contemplating the Beatitudes in the light of esoteric wisdom forges links to the spirit, and to the intentions of the Christ for humanity, regardless of what the Earth itself, on the physical level, may undergo. Such insights become a beacon of light, guiding and nurturing our souls in future times, and in spiritual worlds.

The Beatitudes have inspired, and continue to inspire, millions of Christians around the world. An atmosphere of deep holiness pervades the scene where they are spoken, so they are revered throughout the Christian world.

Over the centuries, countless sermons have been given, and in modern times, large numbers of books have been written about them, inspiring many generations of Christians by pointing out the admonitions in them to be kind, fair-minded, pious, to have good-will to all living creatures, and to so live as to have a joyous existence in the after-life.

But Rudolf Steiner can point out that, despite the deeply sacred quality that Christianity has traditionally perceived in these proclamations, a deeper meaning to these great words has not been cognized by Christian scholars. For mainstream Christian theology, from historical reasons, long ago lost awareness of esoteric teachings in the Gospels, and consequently of a cosmic nature to 'Christ'. There is however, a veiled layer of meaning, of an esoteric kind, in the Greek texts of the Gospels, and in writings of the great third century Church Father, Origenes. But Christian scholars – apart from some mystical, pietistic saints or seers – have not perceived this, and therefore have remained unaware of the deeply esoteric nature of the events in the life of Jesus, which culminated in the Crucifixion and Resurrection.

Since the early 19th century, many academic scholars have attempted to understand the Gospels in a more intellectually precise way than the attitudes which had been current for centuries, and which these scholars now felt to be at times naive or sentimental. This impulse led to the development of various approaches to 'hermeneutics', that is, to analysing the New Testament; this research is called 'Biblical criticism'. Such academic work uses highly discerning analytical skills and scholarly expertise, but is often humanistic in its attitude.

As an academic process, it commenced in the early 19th century, and has yielded really valuable information as to the general background of the cultures in which the life of Jesus took place and from which Gospels were written. These efforts are to be distinguished from the 'spiritual science' method of Rudolf Steiner, which also requires a high intelligence, but in addition, a higher intuitive-spiritual consciousness. He also had an expert grasp of ancient Greek.

We can briefly note here some of the approaches used in this 'Biblical criticism'. 'Textual criticism' examines the many ancient papyri or codices, and fragments of these, to determine which are the most reliable. 'Source criticism' attempts to find the original sources of these texts. Another approach is called 'Redaction criticism', which studies the literary and cultural context of the Gospel narratives. There is also 'Grammatical criticism', which can be divided into sub-categories, for this approach explores the grammatical composition chosen for any text in the Gospels, and then seeks to interpret this choice.

A wide variety of modes of interpretation have arisen, derived from the particular scholar or church's own preferences. The struggle to achieve objectivity in this research has been a demanding and emotionally heated one, because it often has a religious, dogmatic context.

In the modern academic setting these endeavours are generally carried out in the prevailing humanistic mindset of modern times. A struggle to have awareness of sacred esoteric teachings, involving specific dynamics from spiritual realms, has therefore scarcely been present, as this entire aspect is generally not cognized.

As a consequence, there is a lack of awareness of the cosmic and 'mystical' aspects to the nature of Jesus, of 'Christ', and to the purpose behind the events of Golgotha. It is precisely these aspects which Rudolf Steiner's 'spiritual science' approach unveils. His approach of course requires that the student takes seriously what Steiner offers from his knowledge and seership, but his research is also united to a very high intelligence, and knowledge of 'hermeneutics' (of his times). Before we consider Rudolf Steiner's commentaries, we need to briefly note another mode of Biblical criticism, and also my own work in this field.

This mode of Biblical criticism is the 'Form criticism' approach. This is directly opposed to the approach which seeks to cognize deeper spiritual messages, indeed esoteric teachings, placed in the Gospels. It examines the form of the Gospel narratives, as a human reality, by removing all the spiritual elements of the Gospels. Its founder, R. Bultmann (1884-1976), had no acceptance of the spiritual aspect to the Gospels, seeing these merely as myths. He consequently rejected the Resurrection of Jesus, and many other spiritual realities.

Hence in his 'Form criticism' there could be no esoteric, spiritual content, and no influence of any 'Risen Christ'. Another humanistic theologian was Adolf Harnack (1851-1930), who viewed the Gospel of St. John as a spurious fantasy, and rejected the spiritual aspect of life, so he taught that any miraculous Gospel events, such as the healings, were simply illusions.

Rudolf Steiner commented in 1922, "modern theology is actually only a Jesus-theology {*not a Christ-theology*}, indeed no longer a Christian reality"[1]; this is not uniquely a view of Rudolf Steiner, it is held by other thinkers.[2] In what appears to be a reference to Harnack and Bultmann, he commented, "...theology on the one hand denies the Christ, and on the other hand, regards Christ as a myth..."[3] His own spiritual-science research into the Gospels was no doubt intended to reveal those aspects of the Christ-reality which had been so regrettably removed by such theologians.

My own academic studies of ancient Greek New Testament texts, has led me to create a new pathway to assess and understand the New Testament. This could be called the *Initiatory Intention* approach (technically, the 'Initiatory Critical Analysis' path). With this tool, a contemplative engagement with the text is undertaken, in close association

---

[1] GA 211, lecture, 26th March, 1922.
[2] Steiner quotes the Basel theologian F. Overbeck (1837-1905) who wrote a book to support his view.
[3] GA 219, lecture, 3rd Dec, 1922.

with a grammatical assessment, and with understanding that there is a spiritual reality to 'Christ'; a reality which encompasses the living Risen Jesus, and a cosmic Christ-being, as well as a veiled esoteric narrative placed in the Gospels.

An esoteric aspect to Christianity

For those who are not familiar with Rudolf Steiner's view of Christianity, it is important to know that in anthroposophical wisdom, the name 'Jesus' refers to a human being, an immensely holy person; a person whose nature is uniquely divine, as he is spiritually united to the 'Christ'.[4] So, as indicated above, the term 'Christ', when used precisely, refers to a deity, a divine being; a being who was known to the leaders of religions in ancient times, and perceived as the leader of the 'Powers'. This the 'cosmic Christ'.

In the writings of Origenes, there are some passages which present a view of 'Christ' similar to that of Rudolf Steiner. In his commentary on the Gospel of St. John, which survived the fierce destruction of his writings by lesser theologians, Origenes defines 'Christ' as the foremost of the 'Hosts of the Lord Sabaoth': this phrase refers to divine-spiritual beings known as the Powers (in Greek, Exousiai - ἐξουσίαι).[5]

This great spiritual being is understood in anthroposophy, as that same being who is referred to as 'God', at the very start of the Bible, in the Book of Genesis (1:1), "In the beginning, God created Heaven and Earth".[6] Actually, the word 'God' here, in Hebrew, is a plural noun, 'Elohim', and is understood to refer to a plurality of beings, although it is always translated by convention as if only a single deity is meant. In the research of Rudolf Steiner, the 'Christ' then is the foremost of these sublime beings, the Elohim or Powers. So, the Hebrew people at the time of Jesus, when encountering Jesus Christ, were encountering 'God' speaking to them, through Jesus.[7]

---

[4] The passage in the Gospel of John which refers to Jesus as separate from the 'Christ' being, is presented in my *Rudolf Steiner on Leonardo's Last Supper*, and *The Hellenistic Mysteries and Christianity*.

[5] We cannot go into this theme in detail, but the sentence with which the Bible begins, does have the plural 'Elohim' as do quite a number of other passages in the Bible. It is not, as often supposed, a singular noun in the form of a 'royal plural'.

[6] But in the second chapter of Genesis, the word also translated as 'God', in Hebrew, refers to another deity, JHVH, (Jehovah) who is also another, specific member of the Powers.

[7] To avoid complex themes, the zodiacal Logos aspect of the cosmic Christ reality is not discussed here: see my *Rudolf Steiner on Leonardo's Last Supper*.

It is a core truth of anthroposophical understanding of the events of Golgotha, that the cosmic Christ united with the soul (or aura) of the Earth; an event made possible by the sacrificial death of Jesus. So ever since the events of Golgotha, our planet has been permeated, on a spiritual level, by the cosmic Christ. This theme is presented in more detail in my *Rudolf Steiner Handbook.*

Rudolf Steiner points out that the key to understanding the Beatitudes is to realize that these statements, proclaimed by Jesus Christ, are based on a vast, cosmic knowledge of Creation and of the future intentions for humanity held by this Being, the sublime leader of the Powers or Exousiai, 'the cosmic Christ' (or simply, 'the Christ').

The Initiatory Intention approach to New Testament Greek studies is able to confirm that many of the anthroposophical perspectives from Rudolf Steiner are fully supported by the ancient Greek text itself. A new stage in the understanding of the Beatitudes has been made possible through merging academic expertise in the Greek language with a meditative contemplation of Rudolf Steiner's commentary on these proclamations.

In the Initiatory Intention approach to the Gospels, it is understood that editorial work does occur with a writer of the gospels when he is presenting the context of the deeds, and to a lesser extent, the words, of Christ. However, the words of the Beatitudes and of the Lord's Prayer, are regarded as deriving from Christ himself (but translated from Aramaic into Greek, by the Gospel writer).

One stark contrast between the humanistic approach to the Beatitudes themselves, and the Initiatory Critical Analysis approach, with its anthroposophical orientation, needs to be noted here. Many academic scholars regard the Beatitudes not as words proclaimed by Jesus Christ, but as words formulated, primarily or fully by St. Matthew himself, impelled by his social-political-religious convictions. This viewpoint, directly contrary to that of Rudolf Steiner, was signalled in the 1830's, and became fully accepted by many academic theologians in the late 20th century.[8] We shall soon examine the very different understanding as to the origin of the Beatitudes in Rudolf Steiner's work.

---

[8] In the 1840's Prof. Heinrich A.W. Meyer noted another critic had inferred "limiting, later, reflections" existed in the Greek Beatitudes (*Commentary on Gospel of Matthew*, (Vol.1.; 5:4). By 1980, Prof. R. Gundry can write that, "...verses in Isaiah provide the source for the first Beatitude...The fifth Beatitude...Matthew has constructed out of Jesus' teaching on mercy", *Matthew, a Commentary on his Handbook for a Mixed Church under Persecution*, Eerdmans, Michigan, 1982, ps. 67, 70.

We cannot go into all the details of an anthroposophical understanding of the Gospels, but we need to note one significant feature of the anthroposophical view. This is that the Gospel writers are understood to have received inspiration from the Risen Christ, as they wrote their Gospels, giving clarity to their awareness of the events of the three years of the life of Jesus, as they began to contemplate the three years, some years after the Resurrection.

Rudolf Steiner's contribution

All of Rudolf Steiner's published comments on the Beatitudes are included here, together with his commentaries in archive documents. These have been painstakingly restored and translated. His teachings on the Beatitudes were given over some five years, and most of these lectures were eventually published in six books. However two lectures, one recently published, (in volume 90a), the other, which is very brief, from 1904, is still in the Archives. These two talks approach the subject from a different perspective to that of the other lectures. Of the nine occasions when he gave talks on this theme, only one of these lectures had full stenographic notes recorded; the notes of all the others are brief.

So, to give a clear view of what he taught, all of his words extracted from the various lectures shall be presented, for each Beatitude, in sequence, over three chapters, except for the two lectures mentioned above: the one in vol 90a, and the Archive document from 1904. These are reproduced in Chapters Five and Six, because of their different nature.

His spiritual wisdom reveals a previously unknown depth to these statements, made by the cosmic Christ, and how these refer to the future development of humanity. Tremendous cosmic truths, pointing towards the future, are unveiled. To help sincere students of the Christ-Mystery to absorb this deeper perspective on the Beatitudes is why this book was written. It is the result of a quest to understand the Beatitudes from a spiritual viewpoint, inspired by the work of Rudolf Steiner, and a contemplative study of the ancient Greek text.

Towards the end of the book, we shall review the essence of what all these commentaries are saying, and then contemplate this in the light of other esoteric texts or general anthroposophical views.

Among the many gifts of Rudolf Steiner to posterity are his profound explanations of these sayings of Christ Jesus, which form the foundation of an esoteric, cosmic Christianity. The

Beatitudes are much deeper than the non-esoteric, or often humanistic academic viewpoint appreciates. Rudolf Steiner's words enable people to grasp the immensely significant message which the Christ is communicating in these nine statements. St. Matthew recorded these words about humanity's spiritual future.

The understanding of these words is immeasurably deepened, when one views the 'Christ' in the light of Rudolf Steiner's teachings, that is, as a sublime deity: the highest of the Powers or the great 'solar logos', whose inspiring wisdom and divine love flowed through the words of the man, Jesus, whose soul-spiritual nature is permanently linked with that of the deity, the cosmic Christ. By lacking this perspective, which is discreetly supported by the Greek text of the Gospels, the approach to the Gospels by theologians prevents scholars from cognizing the deeper esoteric meanings of these ancient Greek writings.

Religious scholars often view the Beatitudes as another version of the teachings of Jesus recorded by St. Luke (in Chapter 6). This is where some phrases occur which have points of similarity to two or three of the Beatitudes. But, as we shall see, there is evidence to indicate that the words in Luke's Gospel are not connected at all with the Beatitudes. One implication of Rudolf Steiner's understanding of the Beatitudes is that these two events occurred on separate occasions. But above all, his work points out that human nature can be viewed as having nine aspects, and that each Beatitude refers to one of these nine 'members' of the human being. Rudolf Steiner's capacity to understand this esoteric aspect, and to research this in spiritual realms, has opened up an invaluable new aspect to Christianity.

This understanding that there is such an esoteric aspect, is affirmed by the esoteric mystical library of Christian and Gnostic writing found in Nag Hammadi, (Egypt), and also by the Dead Sea Scrolls, which imply a strong Essene link to the disciples. There are also many mystical inter-testamental writings, from about 200 BC to AD 250, which attest to an esoteric view of Christianity. But the primary source for esoteric Christianity is the spiritual research of Rudolf Steiner, who already in 1902, taught that the Essenes were closely linked to both Jesus and the disciples.

The context here is that a marked non-awareness prevails and has always prevailed, amongst theological scholars with regard to the very real, and quite obvious, esoteric aspect of the Gospels. There is evidence in the Gospels that many incidents and sayings of Jesus are actually discreetly conveying esoteric truths. There is also evidence of a collegial working together with Jesus of people involved in an esoteric-initiatory quest; people who in his time, were especially aware of the esoteric-occult realities, and were seeking to be initiated, especially the Essenes.

This situation, that Christian theology for centuries has not been focussed on indications of higher spiritual-esoteric aspects, reflects what Rudolf Steiner explained as a requirement of world destiny, namely that Christianity should lose its esoteric wisdom, and gradually become a humanistic religion, accompanying the journey of the European people into an enhanced sense of self or "I", but a sense of self which would become increasingly earth-focussed. However, as we shall see in the 1905 lecture on the Beatitudes, he taught that this materialistic, non-esoteric phase should now end.

A predominant theological view sees the Gospel writers, in their editorial role of recording many events in the life of Christ, as people who had a mind-set somewhat similar to that of modern theologians. That is, people without any higher consciousness or enhanced intuitive-spiritual faculties, through which higher truths could be directly experienced. But it is these faculties which would allow perception of the deeper aspects of the Christ-Mystery and also enable revelations from higher realms to stream into their soul. In anthroposophical wisdom, it is clear that the evangelists had a capacity for both spiritual insights and for clairvoyant experiences, and that their life's work centred around cognizing the Christ-Mystery from this deeper perspective.

The deeply veiled nature of the Beatitudes is reflected in the fact that, other than Rudolf Steiner, apparently no Christian scholar has ever been able to discern their esoteric meaning; initiatory wisdom of a high degree is needed to do this. Commentaries from prominent thinkers, after the third century, when esoteric understanding of Christianity had faded out, show no awareness of the deeper, esoteric meaning. So this is the case with the writings of John Chrysostom, Augustine, Jerome, Gregory of Nyssa, and others. Gregory established the idea of the Beatitudes as admonitions towards spirituality, which are like rungs in a ladder, which lead the believer ever higher, up to the Divine.

This idea, which has a slight relevance to the deeper meaning of the Beatitudes, is still widely viewed as a valuable viewpoint. The commentaries written on the Beatitudes from such church fathers and theologians, are in effect sermons on morality, viewing the Beatitudes as urging people toward a higher morality and goodness. Which is what they are, but this now has to be understood in a much deeper way, against a larger view of the evolutionary journey of humanity.

Clement of Alexandria and Origenes

In fact, the writings of the most esoterically insightful Christian scholars, from the 2nd and 3rd centuries, namely Clement of Alexandria and his student Origenes, who refers to the cosmic Christ as the foremost of the Powers, also show no knowledge of their esoteric meaning. For example, Origenes, in Book Four of his *First Principles*, refers briefly to the Beatitudes simply as admonitions to a more pious life, to secure a future place in the kingdom of God. And in the fragment which remains of his *Commentary on the Gospel of Matthew* (Book Two), he states "to a person who is...a peace-maker...there is nothing at all in the divine words (the Gospels) which is crooked or perverse....such a person sees an abundance of peace".[9] As scholars remark, this is a very odd and narrow viewpoint, implying that a 'peace-maker' is simply someone to whom there are no serious inconsistencies in the messages of Scripture.

The situation is similar with Clement[10], whose writings include some remarkably esoteric truths, such as stating that 'the Mysteries', that is the Hellenistic initiation rituals, are celebrated in the night-time, because then "the soul has withdrawn from the body". But when writing of the 'meek' in regard to the third Beatitude, Clement primarily specifies 'the meek' as people, "bringing to an end the battle in the soul concerning lack of confidence or lack of perception" (regarding the Gospel message). He also defines these people as souls who have overcome fury and lust, which accords with Rudolf Steiner explanation,[11] but he then defines the 'peace-makers' of Beatitude 7, in a similar way as to 'meek', which is an inadequate view, since two different types of people are obviously meant.

These examples indicate that even these two sages could not perceive the deeper meaning of the Beatitudes. If they could not, then it is only through Rudolf Steiner that the deeper meaning can be learned. But it is possible, in the earlier centuries when some initiatory wisdom still existed amongst Christians, that these two men did have at least some perception of the deeper meaning, but considered it wrong to reveal this in their public writings. For there are little-known comments about the Beatitudes, apparently from

---

[9] In the Greek Philokalia text, "Τούτῳ δὲ τῷ ἑκατέρως εἰρηνοποιῷ οὐδὲν ἐν τοῖς θείοις λογίοις ἔτι ἐστι τοιούτῳ σκολιὸν μηδὲ στπαγγαλῶδες...."
[10] In his *Stromata*, Book 4, chapter 6.
[11] In the Greek of Clement, (...πραεις δέ εἰσιν οἱ τὴν ἄπιστον μαχην τὴν ἐν τῇ ψυχῇ...) in Migne, Tom. 8, ΚΛΗΜΕΝΤΟΣ, p. 1248, 1857.

Origenes, which do indicate awareness of an esoteric meaning. These comments, referred to as 'Catenae', are preserved in the margins of writings by early theologians. Those identified as coming from Origenes may have been an oral tradition, and perhaps originally confidential. Here are his words about the Beatitudes over-all,

> "The words of Christ are the Treasuries of Wisdom which, through these instructions, proclaim from 'the Blessings' (*Beatitudes*), what is of primary importance and relevance to oneself." [12]   (trans. the author)

The phase, 'Treasuries of Wisdom' (*The Thesaurii of Sophia*) has a distinct echo of Hellenistic esoteric literature, such as the Hermetic texts, and the Books of Jeu, which refer to 'Treasuries of Light' existing in spiritual realms.

These rare texts from Origenes have been preserved in old manuscripts, held in various museums or libraries. For this book, I have translated further remarks by Origenes which are relevant to the Beatitudes, as they are otherwise almost unknown: they will be considered later.

Given 'on the mount', not on 'the plain'

The original context of the Beatitudes, as Matthew's Gospel subtly indicates, is that Christ Jesus proclaimed these sublime, esoteric truths to the 12 disciples during a private instruction hour. St. Matthew was one of these 12 disciples, and he experienced these proclamations in their full power. As the only one of these disciples to write a Gospel, some years after the Resurrection, he recalled these truths of this instruction session, and other profound moments of the three years. These were vividly remembered, and their deeper significance perceived. Through the spiritual inspiration of Jesus, the deep significance of the Beatitudes was rayed forth to Matthew's intuitive consciousness (or 'spiritual-soul'), as he worked on the task of sculpting his Gospel.

Whereas, St. Luke had a very different task, and his Gospel has a different orientation; he specifically tells the reader that Jesus on one occasion, when giving some quite extensive

---

[12] A catenae fragment from Origenes preserved and edited by E. Klostermann, Leipzig, in E. Klostermann, *Die Griechischen Christlichen Schriftsteller ...Origenes: zwölfter Band*, Leipzig, 1941. p. 50. The Greek here is: Στόμα Χριστοῦ ἀνοιγομενον ὁι Θησαυροὶ τῆς σοφίας εἰσίν, οὓς προφέρει διὰ τῆς διδασκαλίας, ἀρχόμενοςπρεπόντως αὐτῷ ἀπο τῶν μακαρισμῶν.

teachings, was doing so to **large crowds**, and that Jesus was **standing, on 'the plain'** as he did so.

Now, in regard to St. Matthew's Gospel, scholars have concluded that Jesus was also speaking to a crowd of people. But the Beatitudes were not given to the crowds of people who had been following Jesus. In the 1905 lecture Rudolf Steiner taught, and the original Greek confirms, that Jesus had gone away from the crowds, to "go up the mountain". This phrase is a veiled way of saying that the Beatitudes were given to the Disciples in a private teaching session, for they are profound, esoteric proclamations, comprehensible only to more advanced souls. But St. Matthew was aware that these sayings were to be placed in his Gospel, so that they could in later millennia, be contemplated and understood by souls who acquired some esoteric knowledge (such as that which Rudolf Steiner offers).

Rudolf Steiner is referring to the fact that just before this section in the Gospel where the Beatitudes are recorded, we are told that large crowds had been following Jesus, for whom he had been working healing miracles. But then the next sentence, which is the beginning of the Sermon on the Mount, begins, in the *New International Version* (NIV),

"And, seeing the multitude, he went up into a mountain",
Idoen de tous oxlous anebae eis to oros
('Ιδὼν δὲ τοὺς ὄχλους ἀνέβη εἰς τὸ ὄρος...)

But this sentence is not well translated, because the verb (*idoen*) here implies the past tense, and it is also used for *experiencing* something, thus it really reads,

> "Then, having experienced the crowds, he 'ascended up into the mountain'..."

As we shall soon discover, Rudolf Steiner taught that this phrase is a 'Mystery' phrase, and means that a person is entering into a secretive esoteric sanctuary, wherein higher consciousness could be developed.

And in fact, a properly nuanced translation does imply, as Rudolf Steiner taught, that Jesus left the crowds behind and then "went up the mountain". In fact, there is yet another possibility here, because the Greek verb which is usually translated as "seeing", but translated by me here as "experiencing", has other meanings. This includes 'to be clairvoyantly observing'. So, the sentence is to some extent (deliberately) ambiguous, and hence can also be understood as saying,

"Then, having spiritually (clairvoyantly) observed the crowds, he 'ascended up into the mountain'…"

We need to be aware of the sequence of events and the social context here. We are in only Chapter Five of the Gospel. So just a short time has passed since Jesus had become the vessel of cosmic Christ, at the Baptism in the Jordan, and then as 'Jesus Christ' (Jesus, the vessel of the Christ), had repelled evil powers at the events of the Temptation. He went into Palestine, healing and interacting with many people; soon after this, he gave the Sermon on the Mount.

Both of these possible meanings of the verb are saying: Jesus Christ, who is a kind of 'God-man', deeply contemplated (i.e., clairvoyantly observed) the masses of people amongst whom his mission had been, and would be, unfolding. So then he departed from the crowds, to go into a private esoteric sanctuary, where the 12 Disciples, in a kind of initiation process, would be given understanding of the great, cosmic significance that the advent of the Christ would have for we human beings on the long evolutionary journey lying ahead of us.

Chapter One

The context of the commentaries from Rudolf Steiner

The presentation of the Beatitudes commences with two verses which indicate that Jesus Christ had inwardly assessed the situation of the masses of people, and this activity forms the impetus behind his decision to depart from them, and to go to a private esoteric place, where he could reveal to his Disciples the momentous, far-seeing proclamations about humanity's future, known as, or rather unknown as, the *Beatitudes,* which is how the *Sermon on the Mount* begins.

For we can conclude that Jesus must have departed from the crowds, before giving the Sermon on the Mount as an initiatory event, because he could not have stayed with the crowds, and also departed, to go into a private, esoteric sanctuary. There is an indication that some eastern Christian scholars sensed the phrase 'up on a mountain' somehow meant something special. A Syriac Bishop, Isho'Dad of Merv, wrote in the 9th century, that "the mountain typifies Heaven, to which the righteous {*spiritually advanced*} people can ascend".[13]

Furthermore, St. Matthew especially tells the reader that Jesus **"seated himself"**, (in a private place dedicated to esoteric instruction), and that the Disciples then approached him, to learn from him. To 'be seated' as a phrase in Jewish religious traditions (e.g., the Talmud) is, as scholars are aware,[14] virtually synonymous with 'to teach'. So, to the discerning scholar, St. Matthew has let it be known that Jesus, inside a private sanctuary, had adopted the specific teaching posture used in the Semitic world, and indeed in much of the Orient.

For he is about to instruct them concerning the relationship of human beings to the spiritual world, and to the Christ-being, on into future Ages. In fact, before the Beatitudes are stated, St. Matthew records some five stages of preparation for this event:

---

[13] Isho'Dad of Merv, Bishop of Hadatha, *Commentaries*, Book 3, edit. & transl, M. D. Gibson, vol.1, Cambridge, 1911.
[14] For example, A. Carr, *The Gospel according to St. Matthew*, p. 113. Cambridge Univ. 1894.

Chapter 5:1,2:[15]

1: Then, having clairvoyantly observed the crowds, (*that is, after he gave himself a comprehensive perception of the people's situation*)

2: he 'went up into the mountain' (*he went away into a sanctuary*)

3: Having seated himself (*having taken up the teaching position of a Master; this phrase here in the Greek is especially emphatic*)[16]

4: his disciples then approached him (*i.e., in reverence, as students, ready to learn*)[17]

5: He began to speak, and taught them (*literally, 'he opened his mouth'; emphasizing it is an instruction session*)

In contrast to this, St. Luke (6:20) places Jesus in the midst of a long speech to the crowds whilst standing 'on the plain', speaking about the poor being blessed;[18] there is no reference to these people being poor 'as to the spirit'. We can now see that the widespread theological conclusion, that both Luke and Matthew record the Beatitudes, is based on a misunderstanding. The next theme to explore, so that we have a basis for understanding the actual meaning of the Beatitudes is, how are we to understand the word 'blessed'?

What does 'blessed' mean?
In his commentaries, Rudolf Steiner explains that 'blessed' means **to be permeated by spiritual forces**. Christ uses the word 'blessed' on a number of occasions, apart from the Sermon on the Mount, with the same implication, such as in John 20:29, "Then Jesus told him, 'Because you have seen me,

---

[15] The Greek here is: 1 Ἰδὼν δὲ τοὺς ὄχλους ἀνέβη εἰς τὸ ὄρος, καὶ καθίσαντος αὐτοῦ προσῆλθαν αὐτῷ οἱ μαθηταὶ αὐτοῦ· 2 καὶ ἀνοίξας τὸ στόμα αὐτοῦ ἐδίδασκεν αὐτοὺς λέγων...

[16] It is a 'genitive absolute' construction, which places emphasis upon itself (Technically, it is a clause with both words in the genitive case, one a participle, the other a substantive.)

[17] The verb here is not the simple verb for 'come' or 'approach' (erchomai); it is proserchomai, which adds an additional element.

[18] With the confusion that a non-esoteric approach is subject to, some theologians, attempting to harmonize the two accounts, theorized that Jesus went up a mountain (though there are none in the area) with the crowds, (that meant many sick, crippled people had to toil up there), and he also stood on a flat area, 'a plain', which somehow existed on the mountain side.

you have believed; blessed are those who have not seen and yet have believed'."

Rudolf Steiner's definition is confirmed by such passages as this in John's Gospel, and by the formal definition of 'blessed' (makarios - μακάριος) in Greek literature as "a privileged recipient of divine favour".[19] So, the word 'blessed' describes the state of a human being whose inner nature is in harmony with divine purpose; such a person experiences a higher joy, and a deeper sense of meaning in life, for they have aligned their soul to the intentions that the divine beings have for humanity; so in the aura of a 'blessed' person, divine energies or influences are present. To conclude that the word in the usage by Christ, means 'happiness', as we normally use this word, is to ignore this deeper meaning.

The 'nine-fold' human being
Through the commentaries from Rudolf Steiner, the actual meaning of the Beatitudes can be discerned, and their lofty messages involving a cosmic Christianity becomes evident. As a result, we can discover that the Beatitudes communicate a meaning very relevant to spiritually seeking souls today, of any, or no, religion. So what are these nine 'members' or aspects of human nature to which the Beatitudes correlate ?

1 **the physical body**, in which we live whilst 'incarnate'.

2 **the life-forces** (or 'etheric body'), which maintain the life-processes in the physical body, and convey awareness of all sensory impressions to the soul.

3 **the soul-body itself,** (the 'astral' or starry 'body'), so named in medieval times, because to the seer it has a starry appearance, like the colourful nebula in space.

4 **the emotional capacity** of our soul
(called the 'sentient-soul')

5 **the intellect or logical mind**, of our soul
(called the 'intellectual-soul')

6 **the intuitive, higher mind** of our soul
(called the 'spiritual-soul')

---

[19] Bauer, W., *A Greek-English Lexicon of the New Testament*...entry "μακάριος" 2nd edition, rev., Gingrich/Danker, 1958, Univ. of Chicago.

7 **the Spiritual-self**, the actual spiritual or divine quality of the human being, arising from a chaste, compassionate, selfless heart and a spiritualized thinking, imbued with wisdom. In religious terms, this is 'saintliness'. In the Orient this is known, and is called 'Manas'.

8: **the Life-spirit**, with this element of our nature, we approach an even higher quality of our spiritual potential than 'saintliness'. It arises when, on the basis of the Spiritual-self, divine life-forces appear in our life-forces or 'etheric body'. These confer healing powers and creative capacities on the human being. In the Orient this is known, and is called 'Buddhi'.

9: **the Spirit-human**, here also we approach another higher quality of our spirit, unknown in normal cultural thinking. This very high, but remote, spiritual capacity arises when the divine Will which formed the physical body, as a vessel of our soul, is consciously encountered and integrated. In the Orient this aspect is known, and is called the 'Atma'. As we shall see in the commentaries from Rudolf Steiner, the first Beatitude refers to the physical body; its effect on our consciousness. The following proclamations relate to the rest of our human nature.

The "I" or ego
In the above list, there is no mention of the sense of self, or the "I". This is because a special mention has to be made regarding the ego or "I" or sense of self. In anthroposophical wisdom, the "I" is always a dualistic feature of our consciousness. We have firstly an earthly "I" or personality, but also a higher, potential "I" which exists only in a germinal form, in most human beings. Our earthly "I" is in effect the combined nature of our emotional capacities, our thinking, and our will. So the earthly "I" is in effect the combination of our feelings, thinking and intentions. But the "I" is most clearly manifest in our thinking: if we are not actively, consciously present in any intellectual exercise, the logical processes cease, but this is not the case with our feelings.

Our 'spiritual-soul' or intuitive mind is the higher I, in a preliminary way. The higher I is really fully present when the Spiritual-self is born. The purity of the heart, and clarity of intuitive awareness that this arises from, merges our normal ego-sense into a higher cosmic consciousness (so-called clairvoyance).[20]

A survey of the lectures by Rudolf Steiner

There are nine lectures in which Rudolf Steiner provided his profound commentaries on the Beatitudes, most of which are published in six books in his Complete Works. One of these lectures on the Beatitudes is in the Archives; it is included in this book. Three of the published lectures were entirely devoted to this subject; unfortunately the notes made of these talks by the listeners are only brief.

Six other lectures were on different, but associated themes, and contain some commentary on the Beatitudes, although this is limited to only a few pages in each lecture. These explanations are the only commentaries available from the profound initiatory understanding of Rudolf Steiner, but they revolutionize our understanding of these words of Christ.

The published books, containing six of these lectures, are:

A *Paths of Soul Experiences*, lecture, 2nd Dec. 1909. (GA 58)
B *The Christian Mystery*, lecture (brief notes), 19th Jan. 1907. (GA 97)
C *The Christ-impulse and the Development of Ego-Consciousness*, lecture, 2nd Feb. 1910. (GA 116)
D *The Event of the Reappearing of Christ in the Etheric World*, lecture, 20th Feb. 1910 (brief notes), and a second lecture (brief notes), 15th March, 1910. (GA 118)
E *The Gospel of St. Mathew*, lecture, 9th Sept. 1910. (GA 123)
        (GA is an abbreviation for 'Complete Works' in German)

(F) In addition, a seventh lecture, given in 1905, has just been published (volume 90b). I provide a translation of the complete text of this lecture, (F), in Chapter Six. It is not included in the sources above (A to E), because it approaches the subject in a different way to the other lectures, and hence the extensive introduction Rudolf Steiner gave to explain its different approach needs to be read in its entirety.

(G) An eighth lecture, from 1905, also consists of brief notes only, and was not solely on the subject of the Beatitude. It has only three paragraphs about the Beatitudes; this brief material

---

[20] A much fuller presentation of this is given my *Rudolf Steiner Handbook.*

is added in Chapter Six, as these are similar to the commentary given in the other lecture from 1905.

(**H**) A ninth lecture, from 1904, includes only a few references to the Beatitudes. It exists in manuscript form, and consists of brief notes; all references from this lecture are made available in Chapter Five.

As regards the translation of the Beatitudes, the normal translation of each Beatitude is given first, in the New International Version (NIV) version of the Bible. This is followed by the ancient Greek text, and underneath, a transliteration of the Greek into the letters of our alphabet.

Then there follows my translation, which I have carefully ensured is fully correct not only to the Greek, but also reflects awareness of Rudolf Steiner's insights. Then Rudolf Steiner's translation is given, which often has an inherent commentary inside it, going beyond the actual Greek text. But, as he comments in the 1905 manuscript lecture, in his translations he seeks to be true to the Greek, whilst also seeking to convey the real meaning, (which his initiatory wisdom reveals to him).

In the second part of this book, the complete text of the 1905 manuscript is presented, together with a commentary. In this lecture, Rudolf Steiner approaches the topic from a different perspective to that in the other lectures. In his other commentaries, he relates the Beatitudes to the human self or ego, which can also be referred to as the human "I". To emphasize the huge significance of this small word in the lecture extracts, an extra space is placed before and after "I". Where necessary, when giving the extracts from Rudolf Steiner lectures, I have added explanatory comments or additional words, in *italics*, and in brackets.

The section from the Gospel of St. Matthew where the Beatitudes occur, in the NIV version is this:

Mt 5:1 Now when he saw the crowds, he went up on a mountainside and sat down. His disciples came to him,
Mt 5:2 and he began to teach them, saying:
Mt 5:3 "Blessed are the poor in spirit, for theirs is the kingdom of heaven.
Mt 5:4 Blessed are those who mourn, for they will be comforted.
Mt 5:5 Blessed are the meek, for they will inherit the earth.
Mt 5:6 Blessed are those who hunger and thirst for righteousness, for they will be filled.
Mt 5:7 Blessed are the merciful, for they will be shown

18

mercy.

^{Mt 5:8} Blessed are the pure in heart, for they will see God.

^{Mt 5:9} Blessed are the peacemakers, for they will be called sons of God.

^{Mt 5:10} Blessed are those who are persecuted because of righteousness, for theirs is the kingdom of heaven.

^{Mt 5:11} "Blessed are you when people insult you, persecute you and falsely say all kinds of evil against you because of me.

^{Mt 5:12} Rejoice and be glad, because great is your reward in heaven, for in the same way they persecuted the prophets who were before you."

The change in humanity's consciousness from which Christ proclaimed the Beatitudes

First, we shall consider extracts from two lectures, which provide an invaluable guide to understanding the esoteric reason as to why these proclamations were made. These two extracts refer to a pivotal theme in the anthroposophical understanding of history, of the evolutionary journey of humanity. It is seen as not proceeding in a simple, linear fashion, whereby people become ever more intellectual as the modern era approaches.

Rather, different aspects of our consciousness become the focal point of our experience of ourselves, in different Ages; thus Rudolf Steiner speaks of the Egyptian-Mesopotamian stage during which the emotional, empathetic qualities underpinned the interface we had with the world. Then came the Greco-Latin era, in which the intellectual faculty became enhanced, and determined much of our view of life.

However, there is also another series of Ages which Rudolf Steiner mentions, though less often; this is similar to the Four Ages of the ancient Greeks: gold, silver, brass and iron. In 3,101 BC, a darker phase, a more Earth-bound phase of evolution began; this correlates, to some extent, to the old Grecian "Iron Age". This more earth-bound consciousness has intensified over the centuries, bringing about in recent centuries, a much less holistic consciousness.

Rudolf Steiner refers to this as the small "Kali Yuga" Age, and explains that, as from its inception, people very gradually began to lose the ancient semi-psychic or holistic consciousness which was the common feature of humanity for millennia. We cannot go into extensive details about this concept, except to comment that if one becomes familiar with the attitudes and religion of people from ancient times, it validates Rudolf Steiner's research here. Evidence for a more holistic experience of life, a kind of slight clairvoyance, in earlier times, is often encountered.

As we shall see, it is the fading away of this more spiritually-aware state, and also the possibility for humanity to re-gain such a consciousness in the future that underlies the meaning of the Beatitudes.

Rudolf Steiner lecture extract 1:

We see here a document, which is so magnificent that there is hardly any other document which is so deep. It was formed in accordance with {*understanding of*} the significance of the mighty transitional event which took place as the Christ entered earthly evolution. The old {*small*} Kali Yuga Age {*or Dark Age of Hindu esotericism*} had come to an end {*in 1899*}. This Age, in its smaller phase had begun in 3101 BC...a mighty step forward in the evolving of humanity had been made, in that from their I , humanity had gained the possibility to ascend again towards the spiritual world. Humanity needed the Christ, so to say, because at this point in time people had ascended up to the stage of an earthly I-sense. The descent of the Christ was necessary to prevent the decay of the human I, so that it did not fall out of its own development{*-al potential*}.

(Lecture: 20th Feb. 1910, GA 118)

Rudolf Steiner lecture, extract 2:

....he who founded Christianity summoned his Disciples to the Sermon of the Mount. {*In the Gospel of St. Matthew (5:1), it is written, "Now when he saw the crowds, he went up on a mountainside and sat down. His disciples (then) came to him."*} Therefore this implies {*when the Greek is clearly understood*} that He led them away from the crowds, and up the mountain. But "the mountain" signifies the secret place where the more esoteric truths were taught. The German {*and English*} Bible translation {*Blessed are the poor...*} contains here an enormous error. In truth it is saying, "Blessed are the beggars for the spirit, for they shall find, in their self, the Kingdom of the Heavens."

What did Jesus intend for these 'beggars for the spirit'? He wanted to make them blessed. Only those who were given access to the secrets of the {*esoteric*} temple became a participant in this wisdom {*up till now*}. But the founder of Christianity wanted to have this wisdom carried out into the entire world, {*because*} not only those who were rich in spirit should receive the Grace of {*higher*} wisdom. No, all those who are outside of the Mystery centre, {*temple used for initiation*} and who are beggars for the spirit, are also to find in themselves the Kingdom of the Heavens.

In earlier times, people did encounter these realms through the sacred temple places. But now they should not only encounter the state of being divinely-enfilled {*blessed*} in sacred temples, but should also encounter the Kingdom of the Heavens in their own Self. They are to rise up to the pinnacle {*of the spiritual 'mountain'*} where an harmonious balancing can take place between the changeable, erring human heart and the ever-consistently harmonious laws of the macrocosm.

(Lecture: 23rd Dec. 1903, GA 88)

Chapter Two

Rudolf Steiner's commentaries on Beatitudes 1, 2, & 3

First Beatitude   (concerns the physical body)

St. Matt. 5:3, "Blessed are the poor in spirit, for theirs is the
          Kingdom of Heaven."   (NIV)

Makarioi hoi ptoechoi toe pneumati, hoti autoen estiv hae
basileia toen ouranoen.

Μακάριοι οἱ πτωχοὶ τῷ πνεύματι, ὅτι αὐτῶν ἐστιν ἡ
βασιλεία τῶν οὐρανῶν.

A.A. **"Blessed are the beggars for the spirit, for of their
    self is the Kingdom of the Heavens."**

R. St. **"Blessed are beggars for the spirit, for they shall
    find in their self the Kingdoms of Heaven."**

Note:
The Greek text, as shown in my translation, is saying that the
self – meaning the Higher-self, the eternal "I" – has begun to
exert an influence on the soul; and this "I" is "of", that is, it
derives from, or has the same 'substance' as, the heavenly
realms. It is not actually saying that 'the blessed' have
possession of the heavenly realms, although that could be
seen as an implication.
    Here, with the presentation of Rudolf Steiner's translation
of the first Beatitude, it is important for us to consider the
strong contradiction between how Bible scholars and Rudolf
Steiner understand, and hence translate, this first Beatitude.
As we shall see, Rudolf Steiner translates the Greek as
'beggars for the spirit', and not as 'poor in spirit': and in this
he is entirely correct. So are all the other scholars wrong in
terms of understanding the Greek ? Does it really say, 'poor in
spirit' or 'beggars for the spirit'? In the traditional
translations it is: ^{Mt 5:3} *"Blessed are the poor in spirit, for theirs
is the Kingdom of Heaven.* This is echoed in the Luther version
{translated into English},*"Blessed are the spiritually poor*, for
theirs is the Kingdom of Heaven.   (* 'geistlich arm')*

To theological scholars, the idea that people who are 'beggars' (hence more or less destitute) are spiritually blessed, seems quite wrong. So, this first Beatitude is generally felt to be saying that people who are poor – whether with regard to money, or with regard to their personal development – are blessed. In other words, if a person acknowledges their inner faults, because they feel that they are spiritually (ethically) poor, and keenly feels this, then, in the course of time they shall become a worthy person, and thus shall be granted entrance to Heaven – or, they can feel assured that, here in this world already, Christ has saved them, because they have acknowledged their inner failings. Alternatively, if you live a life of actual poverty, and thus avoid the earthly focus that wealth brings, you shall enter Heaven after death.

But Rudolf Steiner is teaching here that these versions, based on the idea of being 'spiritually poor', which have been of value to the religious life, are not reflecting the deeper meaning of these words of Christ. So is the universal interpretation, "poor in spirit", grammatically wrong? The linguistic fact is this: some of the words here are ambiguous, so scholars world-wide, and Rudolf Steiner, can each have a valid basis, at first, for their different views – but only one view is actually correct. It is all about whether the Greek here can be viewed as "poor in the spirit" or as "beggars": that is, beggars "for" the spirit, (or beggars 'as to' the spirit – which is the same thing).

Well, firstly, the Greek word here (ptoechoi - πτωχοὶ) means both 'the poor' and 'beggars'. Rudolf Steiner knows that this Beatitude is about the searching for the spirit (spirituality) by those human beings who have become aware of an inner lack. That is, a feeling of an inner lack of the spirit; an emptiness feeling which in earlier Ages was never there, because of the old psychic-holistic awareness. So the word 'beggar' should be used; and hence, 'for' (**for** the spirit or 'as to' the spirit), is entirely correct.

This is exactly correct to the Greek word here, because it is written in the 'dative' case, which means, 'for' the spirit, or 'as to' the spirit. This is the straightforward grammatical fact; the little Greek word here (*toe* - τῷ) meaning "for" or "as to" is called a 'dative' case, whereas "in" (which really means 'of') is called the 'possessive' case. The 'possessive' case is not written in the Gospel here. Rudolf Steiner is fully correct.

But we have noted that the word 'beggar' was rejected by the scholars, so they had to use 'poor'. The only reason that theologians have decided on "poor **in** the spirit" is that they have not seen that 'beggar' is meant. Since "poor **for** the spirit" simply does not make sense, they decided, in order to make this phrase sensible, to over-ride the fact that the 'dative' nearly always means 'for' or 'as to', and instead, make it read "in": *Blessed are the poor in spirit....*

Now, although the Greek word (*toe* -τῷ) actually means 'for' or 'as to', there are some rare exceptions. So, the scholars are allowed to interpret the grammar here in an unusual way ('in' instead of 'for'), **but only if** the normal view (the dative case) would be meaningless. But the dative case, 'as to', is entirely meaningful here, once we gain the more comprehensive context that Rudolf Steiner gives: 'beggars as to the spirit'. Therefore, reaching out for the odd, rare usage, "in", is not necessary, and hence is incorrect in terms of the meaning which Christ intends. [21] Exactly the same 'dative' meaning is used by St. Matthew in verse 8, "Blessed are the pure *as to* the heart...", (although this verse is usually translated as "Blessed are the pure *in* the heart..."). This traditional variation is acceptable, as it does not affect the meaning so radically as does the translation of the first Beatitude, 'Blessed are the poor in spirit...".

Actually, Rudolf Steiner is not alone in the choice of 'beggar', for some theologians, including the prominent church Father, Tertullian (about AD 200), conclude that the word does indeed mean 'beggars'. Such theologians believe that it means, 'blessed are those who come towards God, begging for His goodness'. This view actually is a little nearer to the actual esoteric meaning, than the view 'the poor in spirit'.

But in addition, Rudolf Steiner also translates it as "*...for in their Self is....*", whereas the usual translations don't have this word 'self'. Here Rudolf Steiner is again correct, for although the word 'self' is not apparently there, it is actually present inside a Greek word (see footnote for more).[22] However, what is not there in the Greek is, "in", but by deliberately including this word, Rudolf Steiner brings the actual meaning more to life.

---

[21] The Greek word being dative here, means "**for** the spirit", [*toe pneumati* - τῷ πνεύματι], but the dative case is very complex, and here most Bible translators, thinking of 'the poor', are forced to define this phrase as a very rare 'dative of sphere', which does allow it to mean 'poor **in** spirit'. But Rudolf Steiner knew that it is actually the normal, common 'dative of reference', thus meaning, 'for the spirit', or, 'as to' the spirit.

[22] The phrase in the usual versions, "for theirs (is the kingdom....)" (in Greek, ὅτι αὐτῶν - hoti autoen) is also, when considered as an emphatic pronoun, "for, **of** themselves (is the kingdom...)", and all theologians agree the pronoun here is of an emphatic kind; e.g., J. Broadus, *Commentary on Matthew*, p.89.

A brief survey of theological (non-esoteric) interpretations

Many theologians believe that Matthew himself has composed these sentences, or edited them as he took them either from the triumphant words in Isaiah, in Chapter 61, or from unknown sources. In so doing, say modern academic theologians, Matthew turned some Old Testament Jewish texts, from Isaiah and elsewhere, into a series of exhortations.[23] This humanistic understanding of the first Beatitude generally concludes that, it is saying that people living in poverty may rejoice, for they shall be able to participate in spiritual reality, both in the sense of sharing in Christian values and beliefs, and in the after-life, for they have not been attracted to worldly possessions and personal power.

Or, alternatively, these 'poor in spirit' are understood to be the humble people, whose virtue in acknowledging their imperfections grants them access to divine blessing. This is one reason that the Church in earlier centuries emphasized the advantage of a life of poverty and humility. But Rudolf Steiner's research shows that this interpretation is not what is meant, thus highlighting the great difficulties theologians have had over centuries, especially since the Greek word here does not mean 'humble', but either beggar or poor.

Those few theologians who do accept that the word 'beggar' is meant here, naturally interpret this to mean that these people may turn their souls to God, seeking inner richness. This is an interpretation which is going in the right direction, but lacks the needed, larger over-view of humanity's evolution, which puts the unique dynamic pointed at in this Beatitude into the correct time-frame.

The most insightful mainstream comments on the inherent problems with these widespread interpretations comes from the outstanding German New Testament scholar, Ulrich Lux. He points out, on the basis of 'poor in spirit', (not beggars for the spirit) that it might mean, 'poor *voluntarily*', but he points out, that actually the Greek text here is not how this would actually be said in Greek. So, the next possible meaning, Lux identifies, might be 'poor through the activity of the divine spirit', but he shows that this is not how Matthew's own use of Greek would express this idea.

Another possibility says Lux, is that one thinks of 'the spirit' as a metaphysical idea, that is, 'poor as to divine spirit', (which, as we have seen, is in the general direction of what

---

[23] Ulrich Luz, " ...eine Verschiebung des Sinns des Seligpreisungen in Richtung auf das Paränetisches hin", *Das Evangelium Matthäus*, 1/1, EKK, p. 205.

Rudolf Steiner is stating). But, says Luz, voicing precisely the blindness of the conventional humanistic approach to the Gospels, this is just "too alien to the language of the New Testament".

In fact, as my research has established, precisely such 'metaphysical' language is inherent in the Gospels, although discreetly veiled, in accordance with the protocol of the times.

Rudolf Steiner commentaries:

Note:
In his commentary on this first Beatitude, Rudolf Steiner speaks from a central concept in anthroposophy, namely that humanity had a more holistic, or spiritually aware, attitude and a slightly psychic capacity, in earlier Ages. This capacity began to slowly fade, to weaken, and this change became obvious about the time of Christ. It gathered pace in the centuries leading up to the Middle Ages.

The first commentary given here, is from a very early lecture, and is not among the source lectures listed above, for this lecture comments on the first Beatitude only, and presents some further background understanding as to the impetus behind the proclamation of the Beatitudes.

Rudolf Steiner: Lecture, *Theosophy and Christianity,* 4th Jan. 1904. (GA 52)

Christ, like all great sages, had taught his Disciples in the sanctuary, deep inside the temple. But then the Disciples were to carry this wisdom out, all over the world {*in a suitably digestible form*}, after the power and fire of God was enkindled within them {*at the Pentecost event*}, so that those who could behold clairvoyantly, could still believe and become blessed {*spiritually permeated*}. For this reason, he called his own together, right at the beginning {*of his ministry*}, in order to say to them, that not all of them were teachers in the realms of the Spirit, but they could become something else. And this is the deeper sense of the first words of the Sermon on the Mount, "Blessed are those who are beggars for the spirit, for they shall find in themselves the heavenly realms."

When it is correctly translated, it is understood in this way; 'such a correct cognizing is made possible by a living beholding {*a clairvoyant observation*}'. So then those people who are beggars for the spirit, may find their way to the spiritual realms in Heaven, through their unassuming hearts. The Disciples were not to teach the highest {*esoteric*} knowledge; they were to clothe such understanding in plain words. But they themselves were to become 'perfected' {*perfected is the verb used in the Hellenistic culture for being initiated*}.

> (*Now there follows extracts from the lectures listed on page 17.*)

A: Truly, the Christ is the turning point from the old to the new way of perceiving...as John the Baptist taught: "The heavenly realm has drawn near !" This means that the call to 'cognize the world in concepts and ideas' has drawn near. In other words: the human being is no longer dependent upon the old clairvoyance. Rather the human being shall cognize and research the world from out of their own self. And the mightiest impulse for that which the human being from out of his or her own I is to cognize – not from passive 'receivings' – Christ Jesus has given this ....

The human being today is in the condition of being a 'beggar for the spirit'. In earlier times people still had the clairvoyant capacity of perceiving, and were able to gaze into the spiritual world. This is now lost. But the time shall come when the human being shall find a replacement for the old clairvoyance {*that is, a new clairvoyance*}, through the inner power of the I ; through the Word manifesting in his or her inner being.... Oh, they are not un-blessed, they who are beggars for the spirit, because they are spiritually impoverished. Such beggars are blessed, for theirs is **that** which manifests through their own I , through what they can attain through self-consciousness !

These people are {*now*} blessed, for **that** is theirs, namely that which manifests through their own I ; that is to say, what they can attain through their "I" or self-consciousness {*in the sense of a new clairvoyance, a new higher consciousness*}.[24]

B: (no specific comments on the sentence)

C: (takes a longer-term historical perspective)
Un-blessed were those people who through the Dark Age became poor, {*the small Kali Yuga, starting in 3101 BC*}, who

---

[24] This same view is briefly expressed in volume 58, (lect. 2.Dec.1909) and vol. 88 (lect. 21.12.1903.)

became beggars for the spirit. {*For, as this Age began, the old clairvoyance started to fade.*} But **blessed** they can become, after that impulse was given {*through which*} the Christ could penetrate into the human I . The Christ, that Being who could give humanity cognizing of the Spiritual, of the Kingdoms of Heaven. Thus, in regard to humanity becoming poor, there is the highest Christian proclamation: 'Blessed those people can be, who are beggars for the spirit, who no longer receive as a gift the spirit from outside, in accordance with old way of perceiving. "Blessed can they be, when they take into themselves the Christ-impulse – for then through the development of their I , they themselves can **become** the Kingdoms of Heaven !" {*See Chapter Seven for further thoughts on this important last sentence.*}

D 1: In earlier times, the human being was more united with the spiritual world. The {*mystically developed*} human being, through going out of his or her body, was able find the way to the spiritual world. But now, for us to enter the spiritual world, we have to find the point of connection in the I . {*That is, from out of our own enhanced and ennobled sense of self, (i.e., via the spiritual-intuitive soul and the Spiritual-self) the spiritual world is to manifest to our consciousness.*} The impulse to this was given through the mighty Call from the Baptist, and from that of Christ himself; "Alter your soul-state, for the heavenly realm has drawn near ! Ye must now find in yourselves the bond that unites you to the Kingdoms of Heaven." {*Here Rudolf Steiner is combining St. Matt. 3:2, and 4:17, and also freely interpreting the Greek.*}

To those to whom one could really deeply communicate this concept, one could say; "Earlier there was a time when there were human souls who, when they left behind their I , came into a spiritual realm...these people **were realms**; that means, they **became** people who **possessed the spirit**. Then there came a turning point in this situation. Now precisely those people are being called to enter into the heavenly realm who have become beggars for the spirit. They can become people with the Divine within them; 'blessed' they can become, those who are beggars for the spirit. The spiritually poor shall take up into themselves the heavenly realm.

2: To his Disciples, Christ revealed in essence the following: In earlier times, the human being could become permeated by divine forces, in the ecstatic spiritual process. So out of his earthly I-sense, the person was 'blessed', {*that is, permeated by spiritual forces}*, this person had a direct experience of the spiritual world, for which he drew down into himself spiritual energies and also absorbed energies which brought about healing.

But now, so said Christ Jesus to his Disciples, all those persons can be divinely-enfilled *{blessed}* who in their own self permeate themselves with Divine and Christ-energies. That is, anyone who could merge with these energies, as an ego, as an "I". Whereas, in earlier times, before that of Jesus, only those *{few}* people could rise up into the spiritual world, who were en-filled with streams of energies from the spiritual world. Only these people could be 'blessed' and thus be someone who was 'rich as to spirit'. Such a person in ancient times was a clairvoyant, and was a rare person. Most people at the time of Jesus had become 'beggars as to the spirit'. But now those people who seek for the Kingdom of the Heavens *{the spiritual realms}* can find it, if they seek for it in their I . *{That is, if a person endeavours to let their spirituality blossom; let their Spiritual-self arise.}*

....In earlier times, when a person entered into the spiritual world, they had to lightly separate the etheric body from the physical body; so the latter had to be of a special predisposition. *{The physical body no longer has that special predisposition, for it has become more dense, and humanity has been incarnating ever more tightly into the body.}* Therefore Christ Jesus said, with regard to the physical body; Blessed can be the beggars for the spirit, that is to say, those who are poor as to the spirit, for they shall find the heavenly realm, once they have properly developed their physical body, a body which is mastered by the I .

E: "...in olden times people participated in a gazing into the spiritual world. Then, the old clairvoyance offered them the riches of the spiritual world. But now those who, through the ongoing progress in human evolution, can no longer gaze into the spiritual world, have become beggars for the spirit. But the Christ has brought to the world the secret that, forces from the kingdoms of Heaven **can flow into the** I , including the I in the physical-sensory world. Hence those who have lost the old clairvoyance and thus the riches of the spiritual world, can also in their self, experience the Spirit; they can become blest, blessed.

Therefore the great Word could be uttered: 'Blessed from now on are not only those who are rich as to the spirit through the old clairvoyance, but also those who are beggars as to the spirit. For there flows into your I that which we can call the Kingdoms of Heaven, when for you, through Christ, the pathway has been opened'....

For connected to a 'becoming more dense' of the physical body – which is not something that can actually be proven by anatomical studies – is the situation that the human being could no longer be a 'rich person' in regard to the kingdoms of Heaven....but in himself he can now experience the heavenly realms, through that which Christ has brought down to the Earth.

The context of the First Beatitude

The time-frame of people becoming 'beggars for the spirit' is given from various viewpoints in these lectures. When all of the above comments are brought together we find this: Rudolf Steiner is teaching that this condition of a loss of a slight holistic or psychic awareness, started to appear (slightly) as from about 3100 BC, but gradually intensified, being stronger at the time of Jesus. This loss of 'the old clairvoyance', continued to intensify throughout the Medieval period up to our own times. From this dynamic, the modern materialistic attitude derives; and people have ceased to even realize that human consciousness was different in earlier Ages.

Yet, the above commentaries of Rudolf Steiner are also saying that at any time after the advent of Christ, this darkening of consciousness was able to be reversed – for those human beings who have been able to develop spiritually. Not that many souls were able to have a definite spiritual consciousness, until the 20th century, when a noticeable tendency in this direction arose (along with an intensified materialism).

We have noted also Rudolf Steiner's comment, that there is a correlation of this Beatitude to the physical body. The message from the commentaries about this theme is that the person who is seeking to develop spirituality, can work towards their Spiritual-self, despite being much more deeply immersed in the physical body than were earlier human beings.

This is because the effect of the Christ-impulse permeating our planet is such that the higher soul qualities can be developed, within the "I" despite the dampening effect of the physical body. It is precisely the result of meditating, in the manner taught by Rudolf Steiner, that the soul becomes open to inflowing spiritual wisdom, by a slight loosening of its connection to the physical body.

It is the unawareness of the inner poverty or loss of holistic-clairvoyant awareness in contemporary times, which is the state of modern human beings, compared to earlier human beings, that has obscured the real meaning of this Beatitude. The idea of people becoming 'beggars' for a spiritual, higher consciousness was not really understandable. The larger view of human evolution, of how different our consciousness was in earlier ages, enables us to perceive the deeper meaning this Beatitude. (For further contemplations on the deeper esoteric significance of this and the other Beatitudes, see Chapter Seven)

****

Second Beatitude   (concerns the etheric body)

St. Mt. 5:4, Blessed are those who mourn, for they will be
        comforted.   (NIV)

makarioi hoi penthountes, hoti autoi paraklaethaesontai.

μακάριοι ὁι πενθοῦντες, ὅτι αὐτοὶ παρακληθήσονται.

A.A. **Blessed are those who are suffering, for they
      shall be consoled.**

R. St. **"Blessed are those who take pain and sorrow
       upon themselves, for through their self, they
       shall find solace."**

A brief survey of theological (non-esoteric) interpretations
Theological commentaries on the actual significance of this
Beatitude are fairly brief, in contrast to the extensive insights
of Rudolf Steiner. The main point to note here is translating
the Greek as 'to mourn' is too limited, for the Greek word
used also means suffering. As Professor Meyer comments, it
means, "those who are in general suffering and distress".[25]
    There is another subtle point here; the Greek verb used is
unique amongst the Beatitudes, for it implies that the solace
or consoling shall come upon the distressed person, but not
because the person conjures up the solace for themselves.
Rather an external agency brings comfort to them. The reason
for this special kind of verbal form becomes clear in Rudolf
Steiner's commentaries.
    Some theologians have seen a contradiction here with the
words in Matthew 9:15, where Jesus states that the 'wedding
guests' (the Disciples) are to celebrate as long as he (the
bridegroom) is with them.[26] But this is to confuse a personal
specific situation of the Disciples in the lifetime of Jesus, with
a great, cosmic survey of humanity over millennia.

---

[25] Heinrich A.W. Meyer, *Commentary on the Gospel of St. Matthew*, Vol.1,
p.157, T & T Clarke, Edinburgh, 1880.

[26] Davies and Allison, *The Gospel according to Saint Matthew*, 1-7; p.449, ICC,
T & T Clark, London, 1988.

Other theologians have seen a parallel to this Beatitude already existing in the Book of Isaiah, (written ca. 700 BC), where this great prophet (61:2) declares, "The Lord....He has sent me to bind up the brokenhearted...". As Hagner points out, this Hebrew text, when it was translated into Greek (in the Septuagint), reads, "The Lord...He has sent me to comfort those who mourn...".[27] But the Greek of the Beatitude does not follow the Hebrew, for the original Hebrew verb means to 'bind up', not 'to comfort'. Also Isaiah's words refer to the specific, historical-cultural situation of Hebrew people of the time of the prophet, and of a hoped-for joyous state for Israel which was soon to occur.

Rudolf Steiner commentaries:

> **Note:**
> In his commentary on this Beatitude, Rudolf Steiner refers in various ways to what is causing the suffering or lamenting, (the Greek word means both). In some lectures, it is defined as being physical pain in the sense of illnesses and harm to the body, but in other lectures, he describes this as a soul distress caused by one's awareness, on the spiritual path of the lower self. We shall explore this variation after presenting the extracts from his lectures.

A: "Blessed are those who are suffering": the external sense-world causes pain through the way that the human being has placed itself in this external world. {*That is, through the events which have occurred in the evolutionary Ages, such as the "Fall of Man".*} But the time has arrived when the human being shall cognize the remedy for the suffering – once he or she has taken hold of their self-awareness and thus has made active the forces existing within the I . Within their self, they shall find the possibility to give themselves solace in regard to the pain. For the time has arrived where an external source of solace loses its unique significance, because the I is to discover the power, from out of its own inner being, to find the remedy against pain. Hence, 'Blessed are those, who are no longer are able to find in the external world, all that which in earlier times, could be found'.

---

[27] D. Hagner, *Matthew 1-13*, p.92, WBC, Word Books, Dallas, Texts,1993.

B: "Blessed are those who take pain and sorrow upon themselves, for through their self, they shall find solace." {*This sentence appears to be saying that blessed are the people who inwardly work with pain, rather than fully avoid it or fully benumb it.*} Suffering exists in the world as one of the greatest world-riddles. The Greeks referred to this....and Aesop said that the human being is instructed by pain. The Old Testament figure, Job, through all of the suffering to which he was exposed, comes to the conclusion that it ennobles the human being....The human being has to create an organ {*of the soul*}, in order that he can endure suffering. Just as the eye is created through the light, and the ear through sounds, so also does pain and suffering create spiritual organs. The human being {*now, as a result of the deed of Christ*} carries within itself the solace of knowing that he or she can endure suffering. The human being is evolved to a higher stage, through suffering.

C: When in earlier Ages the human being was subject to earthly suffering and earthly pain, then he only needed to call forth that condition in which he was taken {*out of the body*} up to divine-spiritual beings, because in those times he had such an ability in his being. He did not have to suffer, but rather when he entered a suffering condition, he could seek out the condition wherein he was filled with a spiritual or divine element, and he could then in this condition of being away from his {*earthly*} I , find healing from the pain and suffering of the Earth.

{*We note here that these remarks must be referring only to people in higher positions in the Mysteries, or priests in religious cults, who could undertake such esoteric-occult experiences. For in the first commentary regarding the first Beatitude, (page 26) it is stated that this was achieved by an ecstatic out-of-body process, "by the {not so common} clairvoyant". But the initiated priests in the culture did also endeavor to assist their people to obtain some similar help by a 'temple-sleep', wherein a suffering person was helped to receive some spiritual assistance. And in a similar tone, the Beatitudes point to human situations where those people are involved, who are seeking to attain to a higher state of being, if not an actual spiritual way of life.*}

But now the age wherein this condition prevailed had to be designated by Christ Jesus as a time that was actually over. From now on, those people who are no longer able to achieve such an out-of-the body condition when in suffering, are to seek this power within themselves, through the strengthening of their own I : that is, they are to find the Paraclete (Helper) within their own being. Divinely-enfilled {*i.e., blessed*} are those who no longer banish the suffering through an ecstatic raising of the soul up to the Divine, but rather who endure it and strengthen the power of the I through which the person finds the Paraclete; the Paraclete whom people later called the "Holy Spirit", which manifests through the I .

{*'The Paraclete', is a famous New Testament phrase, which is best translated as The Helper or Intercessor. It is used by Christ in the Gospel of John, when he alludes to his death, and promises to send this Being to help humanity. Christ defines this being as the Holy Spirit: Chapt. 14:16,26 & Chapt. 16:7.*}

In the second statement of the Beatitudes, Christ declared that suffering was not to be banished in this old way, but rather endured, so that it becomes a trial or testing time to allow the I to develop that power which it can find in itself: the inner helper, the 'Paraclete'. This meaning is literally present in this second Beatitude, as it contains the word 'Paraclete'. {*The Greek the verb here, 'to be comforted' or 'given solace' (paraklaethaesontai / παρακληθήσονται) when used as a noun, is the term, 'Paraclete'.*}

D 1: Those people who are suffering, when they take up the Christ-impulse shall be 'blessed', that is, they shall have the Divine within. {*When people seek spirituality with sincerity, the Christ-light flows into their aura.*} Through the situation that they are seeking a link to the spiritual world within their I , they shall become healed. Those who in earlier Ages were in angry, tempestuous states because of their passions, were able in these earlier times, to be made calm when they spiritualized themselves through a {*religious-mystical*} ecstatic experience. Now, through the situation that they are able in themselves, in their I , to find the link with the Christ, they can themselves calm their raging passions. {*So this commentary at first refers to distress in the soul of the acolyte in the old Mysteries, at their lower qualities; but then it merges into referring to people of post-Golgotha times, or modern times, who seek spiritual development.*}

2: So in this Beatitude, Christ, in regard to the etheric body said {*in effect*}: "Earlier, the human being could be healed of bodily and soul suffering through rising up into the spiritual world, by means of the ecstatic process. But now, when they are en-filled with God, with the Divine {*are 'blessed'*}, then those people who are enduring suffering, can be healed, be given solace, for they can find in themselves solace, or the basis {*for healing*}".

E: If one wanted to give expression in regard to the new truth {*brought by the Christ*} concerning the etheric body, then one has to say: now, those people who are suffering can not only find solace in that they can go out of their normal earthly self and come into connection with the spiritual world, but if they enter into a new connection with the world, they can find solace in themselves, because a new power has been brought into the etheric body, by Christ.

So, this new truth, spoken from the viewpoint of the etheric body, has to be this: Those who are suffering can now no longer be blessed simply in that they enter a spiritual world, and then in the clairvoyant state, let the streams of the spiritual world flow to them. Rather, if they now 'live-into' the Christ, if they now en-fill themselves with this new truth, they shall experience in themselves the solace for all suffering.

In Chapter Six, the implications of these commentaries from Rudolf Steiner, with the three kinds of suffering implied, are explored in some detail.

****

Third Beatitude   (concerns the astral body)

St. Mt. 5:5 Blessed are the meek, for they will inherit the earth.

makarioi hoi praeis, hoti autoi klaeronomaesousin taen gaen.

μακάριοι οἱ πραεῖς, ὅτι αὐτοὶ κληρονομήσουσιν τὴν γῆν.

A.A. **Blessed are those who are of a gentle and considerate predisposition, for they shall inherit the Earth.**

R. St. **Blessed are those who are of a gentle and calm predisposition, for they shall inherit the Earth.**

A brief survey of non-esoteric interpretations

As with earlier Beatitudes, academics theologians often view a text in the Old Testament as an antecedent to this Beatitude, a text which they believe Matthew has used to formulate his Gospel. In Psalm 37, v.11, the words occur, *"But the meek will inherit the land and enjoy great peace."* The common conclusion that this Beatitude is a quote from the Psalm, is shown to be incompatible with the fact that the Psalm is about how the ancient Hebrews shall finally inherit their promised land. Although the Hebrew word used ('eretz') means both 'land' (of Israel) and 'Earth', the verse in this Psalm is clearly about Israel, not the whole planet.[28] This situation affirms Rudolf Steiner's commentary.

Without the understanding that Rudolf Steiner is able to bring to this Beatitude, much confusion prevails. For example, as Broadus notes,[29] some Christians concluded it meant that as much of the planet Earth as was desired by them, would be given over to them (*by 'the Lord'*); or, that the entire Earth would eventually become the property of Christians.

We need to be clear that the word 'meek' is not appropriate today; the Greek word here (praeis - πραεῖς), usually translated as 'meek', was used to mean gentle, humble and considerate.

---

[28] That St. Paul in Romans (4:13) extends the theme of Abraham inheriting the land area of the future Israel to the entire planet, this is not relevant here, as Paul is not commenting on Psalm 37, but on the permeation of human beings by the Christ-impulse.
[29] J. Broadus, *Commentary on Matthew*, p.90, Kregel Pubs. Michigan, 1990. reprint from 1886.

As Luz points out, 'praeis' was regarded as the opposite kind of soul quality, to 'fury'.[30] In the Book of Number (12:3), Moses is described in older Bibles as "a very meek man, the most meek of all human beings"; it is obvious that he was not a weak person, but a man of great inner strength; hence the word really means, as we have noted, humble, considerate and gentle.

Rudolf Steiner commentaries:

A: Christ Jesus is himself an indicator, {*a signifier*} as to the human I , to the divine part of the human being itself {*i.e., to the Higher-self or eternal I* }, and thereby he is also that which alerts us to this call: 'Receive that which exists in Christ, into your inner being, as a prototype or model for you to emulate in your life. Thereby you shall find the power to incorporate in your being, from life to life, the fruits of earthly existence'. For with regard to the incarnations of human beings, it is important, in the spiritual worlds, that the human being conquers {*i.e., becomes master of*} what can be experienced in earthly existence.

B: Two forces are active in the Earth: on the one side, ego-centric impulses[31], and on the other side, selfless love {*good-will*} and compassion. If a noble form of love is to develop, then ego-centric behaviour has to disappear. Hence sensual love has to develop up to spiritual love {*good-will*}. To be of a gentle predisposition – this is also meant by the third admonition in the booklet, 'Light on the Path': "Before the voice can speak in the presence of the Master, it must have overcome the power to wound." One should encounter everything with a loving mood of soul, so that the voice no longer wounds; then we are 'gentle' in the sense of this third Beatitude. The goal of Earth-evolution is the development of love {*good-will*}; hence {*those people who have*} this quality, shall inherit the earthly realm.

---

[30] Luz, op. cit. *Matthäus...* p. 209.
[31] Literally, here is the word 'ego-ism'; Rudolf Steiner uses this to mean 'egotism' but not in the usual sense of 'conceited' but rather 'selfish', or self-centred, but in the sense of inherently very anti-social, un-loving, and not far removed from being criminally harmful.

C: Every impulse which is in the astral body of the human being: actions, passions, urges and lusts – this has been instinctively guided; guided towards the good when the human being was able to be raised up to good spirit beings. So the inner power to tame the passions and urges, etc, and to purify them, and to bring them into equilibrium, was not derived from the I . But now the time had arrived – so Christ had to proclaim – when the human being, through his or her own self, is to tame and purify, and to bring into equilibrium, the urges, passions and impulses of the astral body. This is the goal for contemporary humanity, a situation which one makes clear by directing attention to the progress of evolution.....

Those people who make tame the urges and desires in their astral body, through the Christ-impulse, are able to be divinely en-filled {*i.e., 'blessed'*}; they bring these qualities into a state of equilibrium. In this way, through themselves, they shall.....receive the Earth as their destiny, that is, inherit it.

D 1: The allotted fate of the mission of the Earth is that its purpose shall be realized by those who moderate their passions, through the I . All those who have these passions shall lose them, in so far as they absorb into their I the Christ. Those who absorb the Christ into their I can become people of equanimity; and these people shall master the {*challenges and mission of*} the Earth.

2: {*Rudolf Steiner repeats the term 'astral body' in these extracts, for emphasis.*}
Earlier, those people in whom were present in the astral body, wild, stormy passions and impulses, could be made mild, in that a calmness, an equilibrium and a purifying influence streamed to them from divine-spirit beings. Now however, by the power of their own I , people are to find the power, through the interweaving influence of Christ, to purify their astral body. The location where the astral body is to be purified, has now become the Earth. Hence the influence which is to impact the astral body has to be described in this way: blessed and divinely en-filled in their astral body can only those people be, who attain this balance, the equanimity; and the fate of these people shall be, as a reward, to receive all solace and all the goodness of the Earth.

E: What has to be said about the astral body? If, in earlier Ages the human being wanted to restrain the emotions, passions and egotism of his astral body, he would gaze up into higher realms and seek power from the heavenly realms. Then processes would be undertaken with him, which killed off the damaging instincts {*lower drives*} of his astral body. But now the time had arrived where the human being, through the deed of Christ, is to receive the power in his or her I , to tame and control the passion and emotions of his astral body. Hence the new truth now regarding the astral body is: 'Blessed are those who are of gentle predisposition through their own self; for they shall become those who inherit the earthly realm.'

Very deep is this third sentence of the Beatitudes....The spiritual beings who have gained influence over human beings {*already in the preceding evolutionary phase, called the Moon Aeon*} are the Luciferic beings; they have also gained a firm foothold, especially in the astral body. As a result the human being can not attain the highest earthly goal, right from the beginning.

The Luciferic beings, as we know, became regressive or retarded beings in the Moon Aeon, and now they keep human beings far from such a high attainment {*prematurely*}, so that we develop on the Earth in the right way. But now that Christ has descended down to the Earth, where the I can be permeated by the Christ-power, the human being can now properly fulfill the purpose of the Earth.

The human being can do this, in that he or she finds the power to rein in the astral body and drive out the Luciferic influences. Therefore one can now say: 'Whoever reins in the astral body, whoever becomes strong enough inwardly not to be driven into fury – unless his I is present in that state – whoever has an equanimity, and is strong in his or her inner being, and is able to control the astral body – that person shall truly attain to the purpose of earth-evolution. Thus you have in the third sentence of the Beatitudes, a formulation which can {only be} understood {fully} through spiritual science. {*This commentary is very dense, and one point in it needs clarification: a spiritually advanced person becoming angry, does **not** have their I subject to a state of fury as such, but rather, to what Homer called 'justified indignation'.*}

The third Beatitude in an expanded translation, from Rudolf Steiner's commentaries:

"Blessed are those who are of a gentle and calm predisposition, for they gain for themselves the purpose of Earth-evolution."

Further thoughts on the third Beatitude:

In source 'B' these crucial words occur: "Hence sensual love has to develop up to spiritual love (good-will). To be of a gentle predisposition – this is also meant by the third admonition in '*Light on the Path*': "Before the voice can speak in the presence of the Master, it must have overcome the power to wound." One can conclude from this, that the task of the Earth phase of our existence is, from the viewpoint of the third Beatitude, to overcome the negative Mars forces which underpin both sensuality and violence. It is these forces which constitute by far the strongest aspect of the lower self.

The energies within our voice are linked with the etheric-astral energies of the throat chakra; this centre is powered by Mars forces. The gentle, calm and considerate person has conquered the dreadful lower Mars forces; both anger and burning sensual desires. But there is, in such a gentle and considerate person, a substantial inner strength; such a person can manifest a justified anger and real courage, when this is socially called for.

Here there is an unspoken, deeply earnest social admonition: the more sensuality and its associated sensual decadence is encouraged, the worse shall be the aggression which such a culture experiences. This esoteric truth is expressed in the book of Hosea (Chapt. 8:7), where it is said in effect, "He who sows the wind, shall reap the whirlwind {*violent storm*}".

****

Chapter Three

The Fourth Beatitude   (concerns the sentient-soul)

St. Mt. 5:6, Blessed are those who hunger and thirst for
    righteousness, for they will be filled.

makarioi hoi peinoentes kai dipsoentes taen
dikaiosounaen, hoti autoi chortasthaesontai.

μακάριοι οἱ πεινῶντες καὶ διψῶντες τὴν δικαιοσύνην,
ὅτι αὐτοὶ χορτασθήσονται.

A.A. **"Blessed are those who hunger and thirst for
    righteousness, for they shall be satiated."**

R. St. **"Blessed are those who feel a hunger and thirst
    for righteousness, for this yearning shall be
    appeased through their own self."**
                    (implied in commentary "C")

Note:
The word, 'righteousness' is now seldom used; it is a
specifically religious word. To be a 'righteousness' person
means, in modern language, to be someone whose will is
'godly', or in harmony with Divine qualities, as presented in
religious books. Hence, Abraham, as a person obedient to the
will of God and as the unique vessel of 'God', (that is, the
Divine), is called 'righteous'. Rudolf Steiner explains that the
word 'righteousness' means to be 'just', 'fair', and 'kind, in a
social sense: and therefore someone in whom good-will exists
for other people and society in general.

A brief survey of non-esoteric interpretations

There is very little said about this Beatitude in Christian
academic studies. The main point discussed in such studies
is, what is really meant by 'righteousness': is it something that
a person achieves, or is it a state bestowed by God? There are
a number of inspiring texts in Scripture about seeking
'righteousness', and how God then responds, helping the soul.

Rudolf Steiner Commentaries:

A: (*only a one-sentence comment, but of profound depth*)
In the I itself a source {*of righteousness*} shall be found, in order that a righteousness may be found, which balances out (*i.e., disempowers*) that which exists in the world as un - righteousness.

B: (*only two sentences recorded, again of profound depth*)
Here, Christ speaks to the Disciples, of the entire significance of deeper, innermost forces of the human soul. Give love to the other person, don't yourselves strive for love {*to come to you*}; then if everyone strives to be loving, such love (good-will) shall become universal {*i.e., widespread, and encompass you, too*}.

C: We now arrive at the I {*in our exploring of the correlation of the Beatitudes to the parts of the human being*}, and we bear in mind that the I exerts its influence in the sentient-soul, in the intellectual soul and in the spiritual-soul. Through this process, what exists in the external world becomes of importance for the human being. Namely that which is to be spread through the world by Christianity: a fraternal love amongst human beings which pours forth a universal, social good-will and fairness.

The sentient-soul feels thirst and hunger, only on the physical level. Through Christianity it must learn to feel this in regard to the spiritual: a hunger and thirst for an all-prevailing social conscience {*good-will and fairness to others*}. Those people, who in this way find the centre of the human being as existing in the {*spiritualizing*} I , they shall, in that they work upon themselves, become at peace, being satisfied (or satiated) in regard to the yearning in their sentient-soul, for an all-prevailing, earthly righteousness.

Divinely-enfilled {*or blessed*} shall be those people who, through the Christ-Impulse, learn to thirst and to hunger for righteousness; for through the strong forces within, they shall find, in that they work towards righteousness in the world, that in themselves, they are {*become*} satiated with this quality.

D 1: The fourth Beatitude, {*which says*} that the human being is not to develop a conscience which is related only to the physical, has to do with the sentient-soul. Those people who hunger and thirst for righteousness, they are now able to become divinely-enfilled or blessed.

2: Whoever truly purifies their sentient-soul and wants to undergo a higher {*spiritual*} development, that person **shall receive a strong influence raying-in from Christ**. He or she shall {*therefore*} detect a thirst in their heart for righteousness, and become divinely-enfilled; and their I shall, in itself, become satiated {*with righteousness*}.

(emphasis mine, AA)

(*The next paragraph begins after Rudolf Steiner has been referring to the Beatitudes in regard to firstly the physical body, then the etheric body and then the astral body.*)
Now, how is the human being to ennoble, to have divinely-enfilled, {*blessed*} the other parts of human nature, through the Christ-nature which is within the soul? This is achieved in that the soul-element, in an earnest and noble sense, is taken hold of by the I-power {*the power of the higher qualities of the I* }, just as the physical world has taken hold of the soul.

Considering now the sentient-soul, we can say: the human being, if the person wants to gradually experience the Christ {*i.e., the beginning of their higher-I*} in themselves, that person has to feel in their sentient-soul an urge which is just as strong as the urge they experience in their body, without being conscious of its inner nature, for what we call hunger and thirst. That is, this person must have a thirst for the {*higher*} soul-element, just as their body hungers and thirsts for food and drink.

What human beings can attain in this way, that is attained through the Christ-power which is indwelling in them: **this** is what was called, in the older style of language, in the broadest sense, a 'thirst for righteousness'. And when such a person permeates their sentient-soul with the Christ-power, then that person can attain to the stage where in themselves the possibility shall be there, to satiate themselves with righteousness.

****

Fifth Beatitude   (concerns the intellectual-soul)

St. Mt. 5:7, Blessed are the merciful, for they will be shown
mercy.

Makarioi hoi eleaemones, hoti autoi eleaethaesontai.

Μακάριοι οἱ ἐλεήμονες, ὅτι ἐλεηθήσονται.

A.A. **"Blessed are the compassionate(merciful), for
they shall receive compassion."**

R. St. **"Blessed are the compassionate(merciful), for
through themselves, they shall receive
compassion."**

> Note:
> The Greek term in this Beatitude, (eleeō - ἐλεέω,
> pronounced "e-le-e-o"; a soft 'e' three times and one
> hard 'o') is used for either mercy or compassion.[32] In
> traditional translations, the word 'mercy' is used. Both
> meanings seem to be implied in this Beatitude. Mercy
> is different from compassion, in that it occurs often in
> a more fraught situation. In particular, when a person
> in authority refrains from ordering that punishment is
> inflicted on someone, even though the law and social
> custom freely allow this to happen.
>
> Rudolf Steiner uses the German word 'Mitleid',
> which means both 'compassion' and 'mercy' – as does
> the Greek word. He is probably referring more to
> 'compassion', than to 'mercy', for practical reasons,
> since it is a less common that people face the dilemma
> of deciding whether to bestow, or to refuse to bestow
> mercy, in a fraught situation.

A brief survey of non-esoteric interpretations

Theological scholars naturally do not see the remarkable,
pivotal implication of this Beatitude, in terms of esoteric
insights, which Rudolf Steiner was able to present.

---

[32] In terms of the cosmic forces behind the elements of our speech; it is
interesting that this word has 'e' three times, a vowel originating from Mars
influences in the soul-body; but here these are all soft in their pronunciation,
not the strong 'eh': as if Mars aggressiveness has been three times softened.

Theologians of course note how mercy or compassion is the subject of both parts of the sentence, but their studies focus on the nature of compassion, and how the Rabbis emphasized in their teaching, the need for mercy and compassion. These scholars will point out that profoundly ethical admonitions exist in Judaism, not only in the Gospels.

Commentaries by these scholars quote such sentences from Hebrew texts as, "Whoever has pity on people, shall have pity from Heaven", or "As long as you are merciful, the Merciful One shall have mercy on you." In addition, words of Jesus from a different part of the Gospel could be quoted, (6:15) "But if you do not forgive people their sins, your Father will not forgive your sins."

However, referring to these noble statements is to miss the actual meaning of the fifth Beatitude, as Rudolf Steiner's commentary makes clear. For this Beatitude is not about how Divine will (or karmic laws, if you prefer) operates with respect to the moral, or immoral, actions of people. It is about something entirely different: what the self-conscious human being can bring about **as a noble spiritual force in the "I", and thus within the interaction between human beings in society**.

Rudolf Steiner commentaries:

A: nil

B: "Blessed are the compassionate, for through themselves, they shall receive compassion." We should feel into {*the soul*} of every other person; then the compassion which we have in us, and which we have given out in our actions to others, shall ray back to us.

C: Now {*with this Beatitude*} we arrive at the intellectual-soul. We have often emphasized that, whereas the I still dully broods in the sentient-soul, it is in the intellectual-soul that it first shines forth as the actual human I . It then becomes fully conscious in the spiritual-soul, and it is there that it first becomes a pure I . So here we have something quite specific: the human I shines forth, namely that element which all human beings have as their common feature: "I". Wherever we encounter a human being, there exists that 'world', which the human being as such, is, and therefore he or she is the same as us, because in their intellectual-soul, the I shines forth.

D 1: What the human being can encounter in the intellectual-soul, this is expressed in the sentence: 'Those people are able to become divinely-enfilled {*blessed*} who are compassionate'. What has to enter the human being's nature, when we rise from the sentient-soul up to the intellectual-soul ? We then first encounter the I . This, the human being has to develop in order to experience himself or herself as an "I", and everyone else as an "I"; {*this is necessary so that*} what lives in the soul is guided from {*the one*} "I" to {*another*} "I". That which passes from one human being to another human being {*in the sense of this Beatitude*}: this has to be the same thing.

So, in grammatical language, the subject and the predicate have to be the same. In the earlier verses of the Beatitude, the subject and the predicate are different from each other. But now we find that in this sentence, which refers to the intellectual-soul, the subject and the predicate are the same: "Blessed are the compassionate, for through themselves, they shall attain compassion."

We see here a document which has such greatness, that there is scarcely another document which is so deep. It has been formed in accordance with that mighty transition, which came about through the {*coming of*} Christ. The {*small*} Kali Yuga, called the Dark Age, had endured for three thousand years. In the smaller sense, the Kali Yuga had commenced in 3101 BC. This is where the closing off of the spiritual world {*to human consciousness*} begins. Before 3101 BC, we find a direct awareness of the spiritual worlds existing. From then on, the spiritual world became ever more dimmed. After Kali Yuga had prevailed 3101 years, that impulse occurred whereby the human being is again being guided into the spiritual world.

By what means could such an impulse happen ? Only in this way: that a God descended down into the physical world. From this event, the start was made towards a returning to the spiritual world. A mighty leap forward in the evolution of humanity came about through the process that humanity had won the possibility to again ascend into the spiritual world, {*except this time*} through the I . Humanity needed the Christ, so to speak, because they had developed up to their I . The descent of Christ was necessary, to prevent this human I from becoming desolate, and thereby fall out of evolution.

2: The I slumbers deeply in the sentient-soul, and first awakes in the intellectual-soul. Since we are sleeping in our sentient-soul, we cannot discern in everyone that which raises the human being up to what makes a person really a human being: the I. {*That is, with our dream-like feelings we cannot make such clear, conscious assessments of life and people, as our thinking does*}.

Before the human being has developed the I in itself, the human being has to allow their sentient-soul to mature, so that the person is able to perceive something there. But when the human being has developed the intellectual-soul, that person can perceive {*more consciously*} the human being next to them. In regard to all the other {*previously mentioned*} members of the human being, we need to remember what was given to us, {*from our environment, both physical and spiritual*} in earlier cycles of evolution. {*They were less developed environments that prevailed when these parts of our inner life were being developed.*}

As from the intellectual-soul stage of development, the soul is able to en-fill itself with that which streams from human being to human being. So, in the sentence structure of the fifth Beatitude, something exceptional has to appear: the subject and the predicate must be the same, because thereby it is to be indicated what the I is developing in itself. Thus: "Whoever develops mercy and compassion, shall find compassion again {*coming to them from others*}."

E: The fifth sentence {*in the Beatitudes*} is especially noteworthy; and this we may well expect. It has to offer us something remarkable: it has to refer to the human intellectual-soul (or 'Gemütsseele'). Now, everyone who has studied my book, *An Outline of Esoteric Science* or my *Theosophy*, knows what is said in these, and what also has been clarified in my lectures over the years. Namely, that the I holds together the three members of the human soul: sentient-soul, intellectual-soul and spiritual-soul. People are aware that the I exists in a dull condition in the sentient-soul, but leaps forth from the intellectual-soul, and that thereby the human being first becomes fully a human being. {*So the human sense of self or "I" is especially manifest in our mind or thinking capacity.*}

As regards the lower members of human nature, even including the sentient-soul, the human being is governed by divine-spiritual Beings; {*from whom influences ray into the human being*} but with the intellectual-soul, the human being becomes its own, distinct being. There the I lights up.

So one has to speak differently for the intellectual-soul, once it has attained the Christ-power, as compared to the lower members. In these lower members, the human being is placed in connection with certain divine Beings, who send their influence into the lower members; that is, into the physical body, etheric body, astral body and also the sentient-soul. What is eventually developed within these lower members as virtues and so on, this is taken up by these divine Beings. But what is developed in the intellectual-soul, once this has developed the Christ-quality, this must be, above all else, a **human** quality. {*That is, a quality which originates consciously from the self, the "I", in the human being.*}

> Note:
> That the astral body is listed as a member unto itself, thus separate from the sentient-soul and the other two souls, is a common source of confusion; see Appendix One where this is explained.

When the human being itself begins to discover (inwardly experience in the course of cultural evolution) the intellectual-soul, then he or she becomes ever less dependent upon the divine-spiritual forces in their environment. So here we have something which relates to the human being itself. As a result, the human being, when he or she absorbs the Christ-power, can develop those virtues which flow from one being to another being of the same kind {*i.e., human beings*}.

These {*higher*} forces are not beseeched from Heaven, to then descend as a reward, rather they {*emanate from a person*} and then return to the same kind of being {*who rayed it forth*}: namely, a human being. We have to perceive that, from the virtues developed by the intellectual-soul, something flows out as it were from us, **in such a way that something of the same nature streams back to us.**

It is remarkable that the fifth sentence of the Beatitudes actually manifests this quality to us. It is different from all of the others in that it says – even though the translations are not especially good, they still don't conceal this reality – "Blessed are the compassionate, for they can obtain compassion !" What streams out, streams back again – just it has to, when understood in the spiritual-scientific sense.

****

Sixth Beatitude   (concerns the spiritual-soul)

St. Mt. 5:8, Blessed are the pure in the heart, for they will see
        God.

makarioi hoi katharoi tae kardia, hoti autoi ton theon
opsontai.

μακάριοι οἱ καθαροὶ τῇ καρδίᾳ, ὅτι αὐτοὶ τὸν θεὸν
ὄψονται.

A.A. **"Blessed are those pure as to the heart,**[33] **for they
        shall spiritually perceive divine being-ness."**

R. St. **"Blessed are those who have purity in their
        hearts, for through themselves, they shall
        behold God."**

A brief survey of non-esoteric interpretations

The conventional commentaries focus on the question of
what is 'purity of heart', and they comment primarily about
the seeing of 'the Divine', as the result of having a vision, and
naturally this is understood as a reality outside of oneself.
Whereas Rudolf Steiner reveals that this Beatitude is more
about the beginning of the higher "I" becoming a reality, and
how this brings to the person some awareness of the Divine
within their sense of "I". There is, in addition, an insightful
commentary from the great third century Church Father,
Origenes, which is presented below.

Rudolf Steiner commentaries:

A: nil

B: "Blessed are those who have purity in their hearts, for
through themselves, they shall behold God." This sentence is
providing guidance for the spiritual path. We are to purify
and cleanse our hearts. The 'eye' which is being referred to in

---

[33] "pure in heart", it is literally, 'pure **as to** the heart'.

this Beatitude, through which we can behold God, is the heart. For this is the organ of the future, not the brain. The heart is to God, what light is to the purified eye.

C: Now we rise up to the work of the I **within the spiritual-soul**. There the I first becomes un-alloyed, there it can become fully aware of itself. {*There the higher "I" arises, free of admixture from intellectuality and desires.*} This situation is very capably expressed in the Sermon on the Mount, in that it says {*in the sixth Beatitude*}: It can only be in the I that divine substance comes into existence in the human being. {*That is*} divinely enfilled {*blessed*}, are those who are pure in their blood, or heart – which is the expression of the I . Blessed are those who do not allow entry {*into their consciousness*} of anything which is not the un-alloyed {*higher*} I , for therein they shall cognize God, they shall behold God !

> **Note to "C"**:
> These brief words from Rudolf Steiner are a meditation in themselves. Firstly they refer to those souls who have worked to acquire a more advanced state of consciousness, a higher ego-sense; and this is what the spiritual-soul actually is. It is the intuitive flashes of insight which signify the presence of spiritual wisdom in the human being. This is what meditation results in (possibly accompanied by psychic-visual images). As this higher ego-state develops, the meditant realizes that this part of their mind, or self-sense, actually has a divine origin; and for this the word 'God' is used in Biblical writings and other texts.
>
> The spiritual-soul is the highest of our normal modes of consciousness. It is the intuitive capacity, which occurs much less frequently in our consciousness than emotions and logical thinking. As I pointed out in the *Rudolf Steiner Handbook*, in the Old Testament, a Hebrew word (Neschamah), for this exists, but occurs only a few times, for references to this rare, intuitive mode of consciousness occur only occasionally in literature. Rudolf Steiner explains that this part of the soul brings an intensified sense of self, and it is only in recent centuries that people are developing this strong ego or sense of "I".

D 1: nil

2: The next sentence in the Beatitudes concerns the spiritual-soul. This soul, the I as purified {*un-alloyed*} I , comes into its developmental process, in that it can {*now*} take up God into itself. This stage occurs when the human being can progress so far that he or she can perceive the drop of the Divine – their "I" – in themselves. {*That is, in their newly formed, higher I, or intuitive capacity.*} Thus he or she can perceive God through the purified spiritual-soul. This sixth Beatitude has to be referring to God-beholding.

The external physical expression of the I and of the spiritual-soul is the physical blood; and the place where this comes to expression especially in the body, is the human heart, as the manifestation of the purified I . Hence Christ spoke thus: "Blessed are the pure in heart, for they shall see God." Thereby in these words is this intimate reality indicated; namely that our heart is the expression of the {*higher*} I ; the divine **in the human being**.

> **Note:**
> The term 'God' here is actually referring to Divine-spiritual realities in general. Rudolf Steiner very rarely uses the term God, instead refers to any of the divine hierarchical beings whose activity is pointed to in the abstract, conventional word 'God'. But since he is here commenting on the Beatitudes, he uses the Biblical language of these proclamations. Note how in some of his commentary, Rudolf Steiner uses the expression 'their God', confirming that the term 'God' used here, actually means one's own spiritual-soul. See Chapter Seven, (p.108) where it is shown that the phrase "see God" is not a precise translation; more accurately it is, "spiritually perceive divine being-ness."

E: We come now the sixth sentence, which refers to the spiritual-soul, to that in the human being where the I has fully imprinted its nature, and where the human being arises up to a new kind of being-ness. We know that precisely in the age when the Christ appeared on Earth, the intellectual-soul had come into manifestation.[34] But now we live in the age when the spiritual-soul is to come to expression, and when the human being is to arise up into the spiritual world. {*That is, the human being is to develop more awareness of the spiritual aspect of creation.*} In the intellectual-soul, the human being becomes more aware of itself, causing the self, the I, to lighten up. But a person fully develops this I in their spiritual-soul, which now again 'rises up' into the spiritual world. {*It has begun to appear as of the 15th century, bringing an enhanced ego-sense, which offers the possibility of a more spiritual, intuitive way of thinking.*}

In that this person pours the I into the spiritual-soul, and there first experiences the I, in that this human being absorbs the Christ-power in himself or herself, then that person has reached the pathway to their God {*i.e., their own divine being-ness*}. This person shall, in that he or she experiences the Christ in their I, and raises this up to the spiritual-soul, arrive at their God {*i.e., the divine-being-ness which is their own higher self*}.

Now it has been said that the expression of the I in the physical body is the blood, and that it has its centre in the heart. For this reason the sixth sentence {*in the Beatitudes*} is expressed here in a manner that accords with the reality, that the I, through the characteristics which it creates in the blood and the heart, can become something that participates in the being-ness of God.

What does this sentence say ? "Blessed are those who are pure in heart, for they shall see God" ! This is not an especially good translation at all, but it suffices for our purpose. In this way, spiritual science can illumine the over-all fabric of these wonderful sentences which Jesus Christ proclaimed to his close Disciples, shortly after he had withstood the Temptation.

Commentary from Origenes of Alexandria (ca. AD 230)

Although portions of the commentary by Origenes on the Gospel of St. Matthew have been lost, Church Fathers in their

---

[34] The Greco-Latin era (747 BC – AD 1413) is the era when the intellectual, rational mode of functioning came into being.

own writings have preserved some of these 'lost' teachings about this Beatitude. Various comments about the Beatitudes have survived from this great spiritually aware theologian. The following comment wonderfully affirms the view of Rudolf Steiner about the heart, (presented in extract "E"),

> God is not spiritually cognized unless the heart is cleansed. Indeed the heart **is** the {*inner*} eye {*of the soul*}[35], whereas the {*physical*} eye is the **external form** of the soul.[36] The physical eye perceives the light, which is, in essence, of the eye's own nature; (unless the eye cannot perceive an object, because it is encountering something not reflecting the light).
> And likewise, the {*ennobled*} soul, {*through its 'eye', the heart*} in fact perceives what is in harmony with its own {*higher*} nature – the Chaste and the Pure {*the Divine*}.[37]　　　　　　　　(transl. the author)

There is much esoteric knowledge in these words; firstly, that the eye is formed by the solar ether, which is also what is responsible for physical light. But in addition, Origenes is saying that the higher, spiritual consciousness (of the Spiritual-soul) perceives the divine, 'Devachanic' realm. For the 'ennobled' soul (by which actually the beginning of the human spirit – Spiritual-soul – is meant) **is itself Devachanic in nature**; and Devachan or the true Heavenly realm is where the Divine beings from whom human beings were created, are manifesting.

****

---

[35] In the Greek: ἡ γὰρ καρδία ὀφθαλμός ἐστιν...
[36] In the Greek: ὁ δὲ ὀφθαλμὸς ἡ φύσις τοῦ νοος.
[37] E. Klostermann, (ref. 9) p. 50.

Chapter Four

Rudolf Steiner's Commentaries on Beatitudes 7, 8 & 9

Seventh Beatitude

St. Mt. 5:9, Blessed are the peacemakers, for they will be
called sons of God.

makaripoi hoi eiraenopoioi, hoti autoi huioi theou
klaethaesontai.

μακάριοι οἱ εἰρηνοποιοί, ὅτι αὐτοὶ υἱοὶ θεοῦ
κληθήσονται.

A.A. **"Blessed are the peacemakers, for 'children of
God' they shall be called."**

R. St. **"Blessed are those who establish peace, for
through themselves, they shall become children
of God."**

A brief survey of the non-esoteric interpretation

Traditionally, theological understanding has approached this
Beatitude in two ways. One is that it points to those who bring
peace about in the world, through careful actions and wise
negotiations. The other view, which is a more mystical or
pietistic one, which does not have to exclude the general
theological view, is that this Beatitude refers to those who
take up the deeper contemplative path, and by thus purifying
and ennobling their souls, exert a subtle influence towards
good-will and peace socially.

Scholars point out that the term 'peace-maker' is unique to
the New Testament. It is also a much stronger word than
'peace-loving', 'peaceful', or 'friendly'. In addition, the term
'shall be *called*' uses a verb (kaleisthai - καλεῖσθαι) which in
this context, implies prestige or respect in society, and that
this capacity is a permanent one, and that these people are

expressly designated as such, by the community.[38] This is why I have translated this Beatitude, *"Blessed are the peacemakers, for 'children of God' they shall be called";* as this more clearly represents the power of this verb.

The use of such a powerful verb is all the more understandable when, from Rudolf Steiner we understand that this Beatitude refers to the development of the chaste Spirit-self {*also called the Spiritual-self*}, which can only arise once the Spiritual-soul has been attained. The Spiritual-self imbues the soul with a deeper peace than any external happiness can bring.

Rudolf Steiner commentaries:

A: nil

B: (only two sentences recorded)
"Blessed are those who establish peace, for through themselves, they shall become children of God." The soul makes its way from God, through the stage of humanity, back to God {*divine being-ness*}. The souls {*who achieved this stage in the past*} were peace-makers, and {*this*} peace led them back to Divine being-ness.

C: Now we come to that part of the Sermon on the Mount which actually is oriented to the Spirit-self, Life-spirit and the Spirit-human. At this stage, the human being itself can no longer be active simply through itself; for now, on this level, the human being has to appeal to the divine-spirit beings who have been brought into a union with the Earth, precisely through the Christ. The human being now has to raise the spiritual gaze up to this renewed spiritual reality. Whereas in earlier ages, strife and disharmony has entered into humanity through the ego-hood stage, and still enters today, it is the case that, through the Christ-impulse, peace is to be poured out over the Earth. And those who take up the Christ-impulse, amongst that portion of humanity which gradually in the future do develop their Spirit-self, shall become (*referred to as*} 'peace-makers'.

---

[38] This is noted by many commentators e.g., Carr, (reference 5), Prof. H.A.W. Meyer, (ref. 17) and A. H. McNeile, *The Gospel according to St. Matthew*, p.53, London, MacMillan Co., 1955.

These people shall become 'children of God' in a new sense; namely that they shall bring down the Spirit from out of spiritual realms. Divinely-enfilled {*or blessed*} are those who, in this way, bring peace or harmony into the world – for this reason are they 'children of God" ! For so must those people be regarded, those who are truly en-filled with a Spirit-self, which is {*intended*} to bring peace and harmony across the Earth.

Note:
We can see here how the pietistic Christian view, that this Beatitude is about how the deepening of the inner life, does contribute to the peace and well-being of society, does have a resonance with the deeper meaning unveiled in these commentaries.

D 1: nil

2: Now, {*in our contemplations on the Beatitudes*}, we shall proceed up to what is higher than the spiritual-soul: to Manas, Buddhi and Atman. Contemporary human beings today can indeed develop the soul parts of human nature, but the higher members, the Spirit-self, Life-spirit and the Spirit-human, can only be developed in the far future. These are not yet able to exist in human beings; the human being has to gaze up to these {*existing in*} higher spiritual beings. The Spirit-self is not yet within the person; in a later age it shall pour itself out over the human being. The human being can not yet fully absorb the Spirit-self in itself. {*The above sentences seem to refer to the general state of humanity, for it is also stated in extract "E" and elsewhere, that those who intensely seek spiritual development can advance their evolution and develop the Spiritual-self, to some extent.*}

In this matter, the human being is only at the beginning of such a development; he or she is only a vessel that can only gradually take this into their being, so to speak. The seventh Beatitude indicates this. The Spirit-self at this stage can only en-warm, or weave through, the human being. The deed of Christ alone brings the Spirit-self down to the Earth, as the power of love and harmony.

Therefore Christ says, "Blessed are those who draw down, as the first of the three spiritual members, the Spirit-self; for they shall become children of God." These words direct the human being's awareness up into higher realms.

E: The following sentences of the Beatitudes relate to the situation that the human being raises its existence up into the higher members of human nature, in that it develops the Spirit-self, Life-spirit and the Spirit-human. For this reason, the later Beatitudes describe only in a general way what the human being shall experience in the future; and this is something which in our times only a few selected people can experience. The seventh Beatitude therefore relates to the Spirit-self: "Blessed are those who draw down the Spirit-self as the first of their spiritual members, for they shall be called the children of God. Into these people the first member of their higher triune {*spiritual*} nature has entered.

****

Eighth Beatitude   (concerns the Life-spirit)

St. Mt. 5:10, Blessed are those who are persecuted because of righteousness, for theirs is the Kingdom of Heaven.

Makarioi hoi dedioegmenoi heneken dikaiosounaes, hoti autoen estin hae basileia toen ouranoen.

Μακάριοι οἱ δεδιωγμένοι ἕνεκεν δικαιοσύνης, ὅτι αὐτῶν ἐστιν ἡ βασιλεία τῶν οὐρανῶν.

A.A. **"Blessed are those who suffer persecution for the sake of righteousness, for of their self is the the Kingdom of the Heavens."**

R. St. **"Blessed are those who are persecuted for righteousness' sake; for in their self they shall find the Kingdom of the Heavens."**

And also:

"Divinely-enfilled or blessed, are those who become persecuted for the sake of righteousness, for they shall be filled in their self with the Life-spirit, with Buddhi, from out of the Kingdom of the Heavens."

> **Note:**
> As with the first Beatitude, the Greek text, as shown in my translation, is saying that the self – meaning the Higher self, the eternal "I" – has begun to develop; and it is "of", that is, it derives from, or has the same 'substance' as, the heavenly realms. Rudolf Steiner's translation is essentially saying the same thing, but as we note below, he has gone slightly beyond the Greek, to clarify the meaning.

A brief survey of non-esoteric interpretations
Theological comment on this Beatitude focuses on the antagonism that was arising against Christians from the very beginning of the church in some areas, and how such a verse would be a comfort for them. To many academic theologians, this Beatitude is a creation of St. Matthew, who was seeking to provide solace and encouragement to fellow Christians.

We also note that this last Beatitude actually reflects the first Beatitude. It is as if a cycle of seven has been completed.

For in both the first Beatitude and in the eighth Beatitude, it is stated "of their self are the heavenly realms" or the Kingdom of the Heavens. See page 91 and 111 for more about this.

Rudolf Steiner commentaries:

A: nil

B: "Blessed are those who suffer persecution for the sake of righteousness, for theirs is the heavenly realm." Jesus Christ requires that human beings set themselves the challenge of fairness and justice, then shall the thirst for this be satisfied. An earthly demand and a heavenly demand are always distinct from each other. {*This brief sentence is in need of further explanation, but none are recorded in the notes.*}

C: Regarding the eighth Beatitude, we need to be clear that of everything which has developed on the Earth, some remnants from earlier times remain behind, into later times. This remnant or left-over part, is in a certain sense, hostile to that which is placed in later times, in a germinal form. What the Christ-impulse brings is placed within and throughout, the entirety of human evolution. But this is not brought all at once; therefore, remnants {*which are not in harmony with the Christ-impulse*} remain of that which had come into existence {*of a non-positive nature*} in earlier ages of humanity's evolution.

Therefore it is necessary, that those who are the first to understand the Christ-impulse, exist firmly on the basis of the Christ-impulse, are inwardly entirely permeated by its power. And if they are inwardly permeated by the power which emanates from the germinal bud which has been brought by the Christ, if they firmly base their life on this foundation, then precisely through this firm, resolute way of being, these people shall be divinely-enfilled {*blessed*}, in the new sense.

Divinely-enfilled are those, who in this new order of things, which is directed by the will of Christ, experience persecution from those who into the present day are a continuation, in their existence, of something from an earlier Age.

D 1: nil

2: {*In the seventh Beatitude*} reference had been made by Christ, to what the future is to bring about: the Spirit-self. But {*in this eighth Beatitude*} those {*who have developed the Spirit-*}

self, and continue on developing the Life-Spirit} shall be ever more contested and attacked, and persecuted by all Powers and Mights. This is indicated in the eighth Beatitude: "Divinely-enfilled or blessed, are those who become persecuted for the sake of righteousness, for they shall be filled in their self with the Life-spirit, with Buddhi, from out of the Kingdom of the Heavens."

E: Now *{regarding the eighth Beatitude}*, it is pointed out in particular that only selected people *{the Elect}* can attain to the stage of developing the Life-Spirit; this shall be those who fully understand what the future is to bring to humanity over-all. That which humanity in the future shall call "the full absorption of the Christ into your inner being", that is, the Life-spirit, is *{now}* a reality for only a few chosen persons. But because they are a few chosen ones *{differing from the normal people}*, the other people cannot understand them, and the result of this is also that they are persecuted.

Therefore, with reference to those whom people persecute in the present age, as isolated representatives of a future type of person, was the sentence spoken *{by Christ}*: "Blessed are those who are persecuted for righteousness' sake; for in their self they shall find the Kingdom of the Heavens."

> **Note:**
> Rudolf Steiner is in effect pointing out that those who have such a divine quality as the Life-spirit, (that is, saints or initiates), are inherently opposed by the ahrimanic powers, who have much influence in earthly realities.

Ninth Beatitude   (concerns the Life-spirit)

St. Mt. 5:11: "Blessed are you when people insult you
          persecute you and falsely say all of manner of evil
          against you, because of me.

Makarioi este hotan oneidisoesin humas kai
dioexoesin kai eipoesin pan poaeron kath humoen
pseudomenoi heneken emou.

Μακάριοί ἐστε ὅταν ὀνειδίσωσιν ὑμᾶς καὶ διώξωσιν
καὶ εἴπωσιν πᾶν πονηρὸν καθ᾽ ὑμῶν (ψευδόμενοι)
ἕνεκεν ἐμοῦ.

A.A. **Blessed are you, when people persecute you and
      falsely say all kinds of evil against you, because
      of me.**

R. St. **"Blessed are you, when people revile you and
      persecute you, for my sake".**

A brief survey of non-esoteric interpretations

As with the eight Beatitude, many theologians also think that
the origin of this last Beatitude comes from the antagonism
that was arising against Christians from the very beginning of
the church, in some areas, and how such a verse would be a
comfort for them. Christians through the centuries have also
applied this Beatitude to those who are suffering persecution
because of their faith.

Rudolf Steiner commentaries:

A: nil

B: "Blessed are you when people insult you, persecute you and
falsely say all kinds of evil against you, because of me."
Christianity should not be confused with other religions....
Christendom must itself **believe in** Christ Jesus, and not only
in the teachings from him. {*In particular this key truth about
the nature of Christ:*} 'The Logos came down to the I-humans;

the Word has become flesh in a human being, and has truly dwelt among us'. All people become blessed in this belief in the One in whom the Logos itself is incorporated. Only one being can say, "Blessed are ye, when for my sake, you are persecuted."

C: And the last sentence of the Beatitudes points directly to the Christ-impulse itself, in that it says to the Disciples: "And divinely-enfilled are ye who are especially called upon to carry the name of Christ into the world !"

D1: nil

2: Following on from the eighth Beatitude, we find then indications about the especial mission of Christ himself, including in the sense that the closest students of Christ can be blessed, when they have to endure persecution for His sake. This is subtly indicating that the Atma or Spirit-human, is connected to this persecution: the Atma, which shall only be made available to us in the far future.

E: The last {*dynamic*} in the Beatitudes is especially indicated; it refers to the most advanced students only {*of Christ*}. It is referring to the ninth member of the human being, the Spirit-human: "Blessed are you, when people revile you and persecute you, for my sake".

Note:
The implication of Rudolf Steiner's commentaries is that this Beatitude is pointing to a people living in a future time (apart from applying to a very few contemporary, high initiates). So it is providing a theme for contemplating the future of human existence and the nature of creation, in particular, the inherent enmity of the earthly sphere to the Divine.

Chapter Five

(*Only brief notes of this talk exist, the following extract contains what Rudolf Steiner taught concerning the Beatitudes. The very brief transcript makes explanatory notes necessary as well as some additional words to make the sentence clear, these are added in brackets, in italics.*)

There are certain expressions which have been used for long ages in all the esoteric schooling centres {*i.e., Mystery Schools*},[39] in order to hide certain realities from the 'profane' {*as people not involved in the initiation process were called in antiquity.*} For example, the phrase "on the mountain". This phrase means the inner sanctum of the temple, where the esoteric schooling centre was located, and where the acolytes of the secret centre were initiated into certain matters. Hence the phrase, "Jesus went up the mountain" meant that he led his Disciples into the inner sanctuary {*i.e., the adytum*} of his Mystery centre, and there he revealed what he otherwise referred to only in pictorial form, {*when speaking*} with the general populace.

The Sermon on the Mount, with its immense and mighty significance, could be presented only to the Disciples, not to the general population: in this way, Jesus guided his Disciples into the innermost truths of his secret teachings. These teachings were secret because they contain immensely significant demands {*on the acolytes' capacity to grasp cosmic dynamics*}.

The first Beatitude already has one of these {*profound cosmic esoteric*} meanings: "Blessed are those who are beggars for the spirit, for they shall find the Kingdom of the Heavens in themselves." To be 'blessed' means to be 'en-souled', {*this is what occurs to those people*} who rise up from the bodily reality into the soul-astral element. {*And now, following on to the second Beatitude, about the thirst for righteousness*}, Such people are craving the spirit, and {*as a consequence*} in their inner being, the heavenly realms are welling forth.

---

[39] The German expression 'Geheimschule' literally means hidden or secret school.

The 3 x 3 Beatitudes make nine in all; and these, through certain ways of working with them, reduce to seven. {*Just as in Rudolf Steiner's book Theosophy, the nine-fold human being reduces to a seven-fold human being*}. Nine is a sacred number. {*That is, a number which correlates to dynamics operative in human beings from the spiritual world*}.

The three properties which correspond to the lower nature of the human being are: yearning, suffering and {*striving for inner*} peace. {*These correlate to the first three Beatitudes.*} Through yearning, one is drawn upwards; through suffering, one gains victory {*over the causes of non-spiritual consciousness*}, and then one arrives at {*a state of inner*} peace.

The second group of qualities, which are of a higher kind, are: righteousness, being compassionate, and a pure heart in which good-will prevails. {*These correlate to the second set of three Beatitudes.*} When we compare {*the nature of*} this second set of three qualities with the first set of three, we discover that the first set refers to the individual person, whereas the second set refers to our fellow human beings.

Then comes the third set of three qualities, these are virtues which lead us up to {*cognition of*} higher beings. Through being patient and tolerant – and this is acquired only through strict self-disciplining – we attain to {*the first of the highest set of three qualities*}: the stage of being 'peace-makers' {*and this relates to the **Seventh** Beatitude; attaining the Spirit-self, the first of the highest set of three qualities*}.

We attain the second of these highest sets of qualities, {*and this relates to the **Eighth** Beatitude*} by being strict with ourselves, in order to endure persecution for the sake of righteousness. Such an acolyte endures each act of persecution for the sake of righteousness. {*Not meaning that one seeks to become a martyr, but rather, such an acolyte has a 'righteousness' or high spirituality in them, and it is inherent in the nature of earthly existence, that such a soul is opposed by the underlying ahrimanic-luciferic forces in the earthly world. One is a 'thorn in the side' to 'the Prince of this world'.*}

The third quality is, {*and this relates to the **Ninth** Beatitude*}: to declare oneself to be a soul who belongs to the Master {*Jesus Christ*}.

These 3 x 3 sets of qualities are precisely set forth in the Beatitudes.

{*Regarding the **second** Beatitude, it means*}, "Blessed are those who are in sufferance, for they shall find in themselves, the way to regain equilibrium."

{*Regarding the **third** Beatitude, it means*}, That person finds inner peace who draws out, and into their self, the riches of the Earth; that is, whatever is to be gathered in from earthly existence. But {*the acolyte is someone*} who does this without eagerly coveting this {*i.e., does this in a non-egotistical way*}.

In the number nine, the Lord saw something rhythmical (*a quality which corresponds to cosmic rhythms*}, and {*in the private initiatory session 'on the mount'*}, He had to imbue the soul of each Disciple with this quality {*through the design and structuring of the nine Beatitudes*}.

****

{*This is the end of the notes taken down of the comments made about the Beatitudes in this lecture.*}

Note:
The above brief notes powerfully affirm that there was an esoteric aspect to the life and teachings of Jesus, including a sacred place where Jesus could instruct his Disciples; a truth which has never been part of normal Christian theology. A revolution in the understanding of the Christ-mystery shall be made possible, once the Gospels are translated with initiatory consciousness.

This 1904 lecture is unique in teaching how the nine Beatitudes has a threefold structure: the personal soul challenges, the spiritual demands regarding wholesome social interaction, and thirdly, the high spiritual stages of advanced discipleship on the initiatory path of the Christ – or cosmic Sun-god Mysteries.

The first set of three, as the other lectures make clear, is firstly, about being interested in spiritual development despite the effect of the densely incarnated state; and then secondly, overcoming the lower urges or causes of suffering in oneself, and thirdly, overcoming the lower Mars forces which allows a gentle, considerate, non-egotistical astral nature to emerge.

The **fourth** Beatitude is about the deep yearning for a fair and kind society to exist. The **fifth** Beatitude is about the challenge of being actively compassionate socially, and how this results in a compassionate attitude being reflected back to oneself. The **sixth** Beatitude teaches that the achievement of a chaste, intuitive spiritual consciousness brings intuitive, even clairvoyant, awareness of the Divine within oneself.

The social aspect of this sixth stage is not immediately clear, but this Beatitude is referring to the spiritual-soul: this member of our soul is an intuitive capacity. Intuition is the power behind our will, behind our decisions, is primarily neither logic, nor emotion, it is an intuitive awareness.

But the will seeks to be active, to be doing something in the world – and thus impacting on the world – and hence the will is inherently about the world around one, and also the other people in the world, and the common future. Also, the spiritual-soul brings a blessing to society, as it bestows higher insights that can be appear in new modalities of healing and artistic creativity, and in other fields of work as well.

The last set of Beatitudes involves the development of the threefold spirit of the human being. The **seventh** Beatitude is about the Spirit-self, which brings about a true inner peace, and also enables a person to have an inner communion with their Angel and other spiritual beings.

The **eighth** Beatitude is referring to the Life-spirit, and the inherent antagonism such high spirituality inevitably arouses in this world. The **ninth** Beatitude is faintly indicating the sublime Spirit-human or Atma state of development. This stage also brings antagonism from the earthly world, but the reason is now not only because of a holiness, but a specific closeness to the Christ.

Chapter Six

The Sermon on the Mount (Lecture, 19th June 1905)

Introduction

The manuscript I have used is just one of several transcripts of the lecture by Rudolf Steiner given on 19th June 1905 in Berlin. The Rudolf Steiner Archives have recently published this lecture in book 90a; the editor in these Archives examined the various transcripts, and he has placed some end-notes in this book, to record variations found in these transcripts.

The English translation I am making available here is based mainly on the transcript which is in my library; there are differences in the version which is offered here, to the official version published in volume 90a of the Complete Works. Those differences occur in the places where I have concluded that my manuscript is more accurate, and hence is to be preferred over the officially published version.

My version differs in a number of places from the official version; this occurs where an obvious mistake in one of the transcripts has been placed in the published lecture as if it were accurate, whilst the obviously correct reading is ignored, and noted only in an end-note.

A striking example of this awkward situation is a sentence in the lecture where we are told that for any human emotion, or attitude, there exist 'polarities', also called 'counter-forms', meaning results or consequences, of an astral nature, in the spiritual world. In my transcript, Rudolf Steiner is quoted as referring to these as 'Pythagorean polarities', but in the official version, where the reading in an inferior transcript is given precedence over other transcripts, these astral polarities are (apparently) called by Rudolf Steiner, '*pathological*' polarities. (!) As the reader will see, if these counter-forms were 'pathological', then the entire, noble dynamic operative in the spiritual world, in response to human spiritual striving, and which underlie the Beatitudes, would in fact, be malignant. Yet it is taught in the lecture that these are a manifestation of the Divine, bringing a blessing to the human being; for it is upon this dynamic that the Beatitudes are based. There are about nine other differences of this kind in my version.

The notes taken by the writers of the transcripts are somewhat brief, so connecting sentences or words are often needed to clarify his statements, or to link one thought to the next. The words added by me, to clarify what is meant in a sentence, are written *in italics*, and clearly placed inside italic brackets, like this { }.

Also, I have added some paragraphs of Notes within the lecture, wherever a commentary or a longer remark is needed. These are clearly placed in paragraphs, separated from the flow of Rudolf Steiner's words, and **are written in a different font**, and identified as 'Notes'.

By the end of the third century, when much effort was being placed in establishing the beliefs of the Christian religion, and gaining clarity about its main teachings, there was no agreed-upon interpretation of the Beatitudes; neither is there to this day. Though these nine pronouncements are short, and fairly simple in their structure, their meaning remains unclear to Christian thinkers. As we noted earlier, the academic research of Bible scholars, is carried out in the context of the prevailing exoteric, or non-initiatory, context. But in this remarkable lecture, the first ever given by Rudolf Steiner entirely on this subject, he speaks from initiation consciousness, to illumine these sayings. In this lecture, the Beatitudes are explained in quite a different way to his other lectures on these sayings.

As we have seen in the first part of this book, in the lectures given a few years later, Rudolf Steiner gave a view of their messages as prophetic announcements as to what humanity may achieve from the time of the Mystery of Golgotha onwards. And we have noted the Beatitudes correlate to the nine parts of the human being. By contrast, in this lecture, Rudolf Steiner takes the perspective that the spiritual attainments referred to in the Beatitudes, which the quest for spirituality in earthly life can bring about, are already coming into existence, in one's Higher-self, as a counterpart to the dynamics the earthly self is experiencing; even if at first only to a small degree.

Lecture by Rudolf Steiner

The person who knows how to interpret the signs of the times, knows that we are about to experience momentous events. {*This appears to be a reference to the Reappearing of Jesus in the ethers, inspiring and helping people.*} In such a time, it is necessary that higher thoughts and ideals shine forth over the perspective on life given by earthly intelligence. It is from this understanding that today we want to consider an important section of the Bible: *the Sermon on the Mount.*

Without the Sermon on the Mount, one cannot understand Christianity; it is not without purpose that it is placed towards the beginning of the Gospel. But in fact, this sermon, like so much else in the Gospels, is not only misunderstood, it is also not even really known. And this 'not really knowing' such an important episode in the Gospel is a situation which comes from the fact that not even a trace of a spiritual-esoteric comprehension of the deep Christian truths can be found amongst the scholars, and the theologians.

We need to be clear concerning such comprehension, if we seek to understand something like the Sermon on the Mount: namely that the prosaic, philistine comprehension {*that is, of modern academic theological Christianity*}, which today prevails regarding such documents, does not correspond to the true {*esoteric*} Christianity. This {*esoteric approach is from a*} kind of understanding, which neither a normal Christian {*thinker*} nor a writer of the so-called French Morality movement has ever had:[40] for such philistine Christian understanding would never have possessed the power which Christianity itself has had. This is a power which has been actively exerting its influence over centuries. Such an enduring power can only have a hidden fountain as its origin. And today we want to disclose this hidden power in regard to the Sermon on the Mount.

This misunderstanding of the Bible {*in usual exoteric Christianity*} derives in part from the fact that we don't have a proper translation of the Bible; thus the most basic requirement for a proper understanding is missing. People say, "The letter kills, but the Spirit brings life", and from

---

[40] The French Moralists were various writers who continued the impetus of Montaigne, contemplating and writing about ethics, often coining brief expressive phrases (or aphorisms). Those who were religious would write pious Christian works but with that age-old undefined, unclear view of the deep themes presented in the New Testament which had become the accepted attitude in exoteric Christianity. For example, "Oh admirable counsel of uncreated Wisdom, who deprives the humanity of Christ of his own human person, in order to give him a divine person." (Pierre de Berulle)

{*using this saying in a wrong, self-centred way,*} each person can do something favourable for themselves: he or she can explain the meaning of a text, from out of one's fantastical viewpoint. Hence all manner of arbitrary ideas abound {*in theology*}. Actually, one has to first recognize the letters {*that is, the underlying spiritual orientation of the Gospels*}. One has to perceive {*the veiled, esoteric message*} which is written there: in this way one will not value one's own banality more than the 'letters', which one has made into dead letters.

Only after one has understood the letters that make up the words, can one venture to undertake to say something about the spiritual aspect of the subject. So, today, it is a matter of firstly, understanding the letters, and then secondly, interpreting these letters in the correct way {*by finding the primary, underlying orientation of the writer, so that one can read the words*}.

To speak about the theological view of the Sermon on the Mount, is not necessary today. One knows this from the sermons given about it, and we would not actually make much progress if we wanted to specifically mention some of these sermons. Together with the theological understanding of the Sermon on the Mount, there is also a so-called 'Liberal Theology' viewpoint, which has its origin in a philistine system of ethics and morality.

This philistine viewpoint is found in the book, "*What did Jesus teach?*" by W. Kirchbach.[41] This writer, who indeed has the merit of making better translations {*than in the Luther Bible*}, is however filled with a snobbish attitude in regard to his views. Also, he has such non-understanding with regard to the hidden, spiritual depths, that error upon error could be piled up, if one wanted to give oneself up to this 'fishing around'[42] {*in the Gospels*} from the Liberal Theology perspective.

If one seeks to penetrate deeper into the Bible, one has to be aware of the underlying ideas in it; these allow such a book to be understood. You see, the Bible is a thoroughly **esoteric** book, and if I now explain to you what depths are to be found in the 13th chapter of the Gospel of St. John, then you shall be still more aware as to what depths we have before us in the Bible.

---

[41] Wolfgang Kirchbach b.1857 – d.1906. His various humanistic conclusions include that Jesus was a kind of Epicurean person, to whom "eternal life" meant only a (better) existence in this world: the significant speech of Jesus in Matt. 23 is simply an expression of patriotic feelings for Galilee.

[42] The expression used here is literally 'fish-catching' (Fischfang).

It is thoroughly irrelevant if those who have gathered some concepts from the so-called Liberal Theology worldview, tell us now all kinds of things about such sentences as are found in the Sermon on the Mount. For in doing this, such people don't take into consideration at all how much prosaic and philistine material they are giving out, with their pre-conceived ideas, when they approach these lofty truths.

As you know, the first sentence of the Sermon on the Mount is usually translated as; "*Blessed are the poor in spirit, for theirs is the Kingdom of the Heavens.*" Any deeper, esoteric, view of this sentence has to directly confront the explanation which is usually applied to this sentence in the Sermon of the Mount. In this usual translation, it is to be understood as {*referring to*} an entirely normal kind of reward process, occurring for those who are 'spiritually poor'. If we allow this sentence to approach us in this normal view, then it is all about receiving a reward for spiritual poverty and compassion, and so on.

That means that we then are to believe that the founder of the Christian religion has said, in effect, "If you be compassionate and peace-seeking, then you shall be rewarded for this". I mean, {*if this is really what the sentence means,*} then Jesus would thus have to praise as 'blessed', all haggling by people for a reward {*in any kind of situation*}. Such a praising of any ethical crowing from the rooftops made by someone {*for which that person is then rewarded*} – for this, no particular {*high ethical*} teaching is needed, {*especially not*} a teaching which had the hidden power to endure throughout the centuries, and which still retains this power.

One can be clear about the fact that such teachings as that of the Sermon on the Mount, has been given by an Initiate.[43] Already at the beginning of the Sermon on the Mount it is indicated sufficiently that here we have to do with **esoteric** precepts. In the majority of esoteric texts, the expression is found, "the Master led his students up the mountain"; that is, he spoke with them about the most esoterically private matters, about truths which are quite separate from everyday life.

So, what occurred {*in the Sermon on the Mount*} was not a sermon for the general people. Those who can read attentively can find out, even in the translation by Luther,[44] that the Sermon on the Mount was not a sermon for the general people. For in the New Testament, it usually says,

---

[43] A different manuscript adds here, "and makes oneself an initiate."
[44] Rudolf Steiner did not regard the Luther translation as having a high level of intuitive-spiritual nuances.

"And seeing the multitude, he went up onto a mountain"; but in the original {*Greek*} text, it is made clear that Jesus departed from the masses of people {*to go up into the mountain*}.

He went with his disciples to the initiation place, and there he entrusted them with deep teachings, which only they could understand, as they were already initiated and inwardly united with him. The expression, "go up the mountain" you can find in all Mystery writings.[45] The Gospel tells us that Jesus went with his Disciples to the place of Initiation, and that there he entrusted the deep teachings to them.

{*Let me repeat;*} Teachings that only they could understand, being as they were, already initiated and deeply inwardly united to him. To "lead {*students*} up to the mountain", you can find in all texts from the Mysteries. It means to withdraw to a place where the intimate truths about the soul can be discussed.

> Note:
> In the repetition that Rudolf Steiner makes here, we are given a very important revelation about the Sermon on the Mount, which we explored in the beginning of this book. It was not given to masses of people up on a literal mountain, despite many centuries of Christians quite naturally visualizing that this is what happened. Though many moving and sincere paintings exist of such a scene, it is actually even better when people who consider themselves to be Christian, visualize Jesus speaking to the selected, initiated Disciples, about transcendental truths, which communicate profound secrets of humanity's pathway.
>
> In this way, these more advanced souls can be guided by such revelations, and also find ways to let this wisdom gradually inspire many souls.

(Lecture continues)

Let us now proceed on this understanding, that Christ Jesus communicated deep truths, which were not intended for the

---

[45] To go up a mountain is very common in spiritual texts; there are many references to a sacred mountain, too. The German phrase might also mean, 'to lead on up the mountain', implying taking others with you; examples of this are not as well known.

masses, but for the hearts of those who were initiated: that is, his students. In this way they could, {*in turn*}, let these truths ray forth to the masses, and {*thereby*} enter into the hearts of other souls.

Now let's place ourselves in this viewpoint, entirely without any fanatical attitudes, but rather entirely objectively, on the foundation of all of those teachings, which we have heard in the many lectures given here. Now, I have to recapitulate to some extent, that which those who have attended my lectures on the Astral realm and Devachan and the Fourth Dimension, already know. But we do want to let these important truths come to the attention of our minds once more.

You know that we have spoken about entering into a higher realm, in which we find the causes of the effects which we perceive in the sensory world. In this same higher realm there exists our own Higher-self. The lower, {*earthly*} self belongs to the sensory world, the place of everyday work.

> {Note: the expression 'lower self' in this lecture means, not the unethical qualities or Lower-self, but simply the earthly self, in contrast to the Higher-self. So 'earthly self' shall now be used instead of 'lower self'.}

Through these two sentences: "*Blessed are the poor in spirit, for theirs is the Kingdom of the Heavens.*" there is being explained to us, what we have to achieve in our Age, in our nation {*whichever nation that might be*}.

Also {*it is helpful to note here that*} what Christianity calls the "spirit world" or "Heaven", or the "Kingdom of Heaven", is the same as what in Theosophy we call the "Spiritual world". In this realm our Higher-self rests. It is this which we have to come to know; to this Higher-self we have to raise ourselves.

And in that we enter the astral and higher realms, this places us before our Higher-self, when we learn to cognize it. Our Higher-self in the first instance, is something quite different to what we have become used to, according to our mental habits, in normal life.

I have pointed out that when a person, as an esotericist, finds these realms opened, he or she has to first learn to behold the things there, and to recognize them in their reality. A simple example of this is the following: one has to learn to see a number as if in a mirror-image. So, an initiated esoteric student, who is shown by the teacher the number 561 {*as an astral form*}, has to read, as in a mirror, '165'.We also know that such a clairvoyant sees a hill or a cube as if one was inside this, and is gazing out {*towards its periphery*}.

You also know {*from earlier lectures*} that in the other realms, time runs in reverse. We are accustomed to visualize time to ourselves as it appears to our senses; but in the astral realm, this is reversed. Therefore, we have to first become accustomed to the situation, in order to see correctly what we see in reverse. So, in the higher realm, we have to first learn to read.

Also the moral element presents itself in this reversed way. You can best experience this through any pathological example, where a human being suddenly has the astral realm open up to them. There are many people who occupy themselves with {*striving to*} attain this experience. This arises because, although materialism today has seized hold of many groups of people, the need to behold the spirit is deeply seated in the human soul. So, often the spirit opens itself precisely to those people who are entirely surrounded by the material world; their inner eye opens {*suddenly*}.

Then the person is often drawn into a state of anxiety or severe confusion. Because everything which streams forth from us, everything which lies at the foundations of our soul, whether it be lowly, or the usual, or even filled with a higher enthusiasm, all appears in pictorial form, as a mirror-image of the earthly self, in the astral {*substance*} around about one.

There the new seer beholds, as in a great painting, his or her lower self, and everything which lies at the base of the soul. Then this person experiences fear, for seeing all of that is not a small matter. This clairvoyant seeing declares {*to the new seer*} a great, a terrible, truth, and from this there is no running away, no cloak, in which to wrap it.[46]

In the Indian world-view, one calls our physical world an illusion, and this is not without some validity, although this is not the theosophical view. {*But with regard to self-knowledge*}, The human being can easily {*harbour an illusion and*} deceive himself or herself about this hidden part of the soul. A person often does deceive herself or himself about the tormenting afflictions of his or her own inner nature.

But the esoteric student finds everything which is lying there in their soul is {*precisely*} that which gives to them the most intimately revealing expressions of their countenance: that is, once they have entered into this world {*the hidden*}

---

[46] These brief words refer to the serious outcome of encountering, still unprepared, the lower self or the Double. Once this occurs, in the right way, unless it was only a brief encounter, then the meditant, now clairvoyant, is always aware of their lower forces.

depths of their own astral nature}. {*It is because of this process*} that people speak of the serious earnestness, of the sense of dignity, belonging to the {*initiated*} esoteric student.

{*This paragraph is saying that the initiated student, that is, one who has sufficient clairvoyance, beholds, with the help of the Guardian of the Threshold, his or her Luciferic and Ahrimanic qualities, represented in an astral image. And furthermore, people who have discernment, when looking at such an initiated student, can see the awareness in this student of these lower qualities, because these are reflected subtly in their various facial expressions.*}

For there is nothing of a capricious, fanciful quality there: such a person {*who has crossed the threshold, and perceived their own soul*} has advanced far beyond all fantasizing and mystical reveries. In fact, before they reached this stage, the strictest ordeals were placed before the prudent intelligence of the student, so that he or she did not give way to delusory ideas. The student of the modern initiation path is only then led into the astral realm, when they understand this realm. For if one were to suddenly enter it, one would not understand it. However, as I said earlier, such a sudden entry into it is possible in pathological cases.

Now, we see this characteristic of the astral realm: that initially one has before one, the counter-images of things {*the phrase 'mirror-image' or 'counter-image' appears in some instances in this lecture, to mean a **complementary** astral-form, or astral 'consequence' of an earthly soul-state*}. What one experiences in the higher realms has a relation to what we perceive in the sensory world, similar in nature to the contrast of negative to positive, or of warmth to coldness.

But this counter-image {*complementary form*}, in the astral realm, is not due to an arbitrary connection, but rather it is something necessary, like a law of nature. Every seer who knows the connection of these two realms, from his or her own experience, can tell you that a thing in the one realm necessarily draws its astral mirror-image after it, in the other world.

{*For example*} **Yearning** in the physical world has, as its outcome {*or counter-part*} in the astral realm, **fulfilment** {*in the spiritual, which shall at some future time become the actual situation for the earthly self*}. {*And another example is*} **Compassion** constitutes the one aspect – whilst **purity of divine-spiritual perceiving** {*truly reliable seership*} is the astral 'counter-part' {*to being compassionate*}. I could mention various other examples of these Pythagorean[47] counter-parts along these lines, from which you would be able to perceive and realize that everything which exists in our soul, appears in its counter-image, in the astral world.[48]

I am actually in this, my earthly-self, a human being who is in need of the truth, of enlightenment. If I have **yearning** for the truth, then for the clairvoyant observer, my yearning is reflected, there, {*in the astral realm*}, **as fulfilment in the Higher-self**. What the earthly self yearns for, attracts,[49] {*i.e., brings into being, and in relation to itself*} through necessity, the complementary form in the spiritual world. Just as when we rub a glass stick, we generate positive and negative electricity, so does the astral realm manifest the counter-image of the physical world.

However, whether the fulfilment is actually attained in this life {*for the normal, earthly self*}, or only in another, later life, is another matter. But what is yearning **here**, for the earthly self, is {*over **there***}, fulfilment, for the Higher-self; and {hence} this, which soars upwards out of the earthly self {*from its yearning*} into the Higher-self, **this** shall find fulfilment on a higher plane.[50] That this is the truth, was the deep wisdom which Christ Jesus conveyed to his closest Disciples in the Sermon on the Mount; that is, in an initiatory instruction lesson. In such a text as the Bible, we know that we should aim to consider the words much more exactly than is normally the case.

"*Blessed are*" what does that mean actually ? People make very little effort to work this out in their minds. But people

---

[47] This is the serious difference between my manuscript and the official book, mentioned at the beginning of the chapter. It reads "pathological polarities"; but the reading in the manuscript which I used, is obviously the correct version: it has "Pythagorean" (*pythagoräischen*) polarities (or counterparts). If these counter-parts were 'pathological', then the entire point of the lecture would be made into nonsense. As I noted earlier, the entire spiritual dynamic operative in spirit realms – as a manifestation of the Divine bringing a blessing to the human being (and upon which the Beatitudes are based) – would then be in fact, malignant.

[48] The idea of a 'counter-part' to various things in creation is to be found in Pythagorean ideas; e.g., counter-parts to musical scales and to celestial bodies, but not necessarily to soul qualities.

[49] The Archives edition reads here: "what the earthy self yearns for, announces/declares (*anzeigen*) through necessity, the mirror-image...". But the verb in my manuscript is *anzeihen*, and hence means "**attracts** (or brings into being) through necessity...". This latter reading is to be preferred.

[50] The version decided upon by the Archives, reads: "and this which soars upwards out of the earthly self, **as fulfilment**, that becomes **yearning** on the higher plane." But, in this lecture it has been made clear that fulfilment does not arise from the earthly self; rather it forms in higher realms, as a result of the energies created by the yearning down here, by the earthly self.

who have esoteric knowledge have always known what it means, and Johann Wolfgang von Goethe, who is to be regarded as one of the genuine and true esotericists, knew very well what this word signifies.

Consequently, in the second part of his novel, *Wilhelm Meister*, the awakening of the Higher-self in a person, even if not in the highest degree, he called "Makaria" – 'the one shown to be blessed'. {*The Greek word 'Makaria'* (Μακαρία) *means 'blessed'*.} And Goethe describes for us the inner nature of this blessed personality in a way which has to be taken very much in earnest. Even though Goethe presents these matters with a certain sense of humour, any person who understands these spiritual truths, knows how earnestly one needs to read the fifteenth chapter of *Wilhelm Meister's Journeyman Years*.

If only the Goethe scholars would decide for once, to take earnestly what Goethe declared not so solemnly, in so many places![51] The fifteenth chapter begins,

> Makarie finds herself in a relation to our solar system which one scarcely dares to mention. She sheltered {*within herself*}, in her soul's mind, the solar system; in her power of imagination she did not only see it, rather **she was a part of this**. She saw herself as drawn forth into those heavenly spheres, but in an entirely special way. Since her childhood she wandered around the sun, and in fact, as one now discovered, in a spiral form, moving ever further from the centre and circling around the outer regions.

This is all so naturally {and *lightly*} spoken {*as if it is merely fantasy*}, the only way it can be declared, exoterically. But the expert in this theme is aware that Goethe knew and understood what a 'blessed personality' could be called: namely a personality who has awakened their inner-self; someone who can begin to undertake something with their Spiritual-self.[52] This Spiritual-self arises for us as a consequence in the 'realm of mirrored-reflections' {*counter-*

---

[51] The version decided upon in the Archives book reads: "...what Goethe declared in so many places **really** seriously..." (*recht ernst*). But my manuscript has: "...what Goethe declared in so many places not so solemnly" (*nicht ernst*). This reading is to be preferred, since Rudolf Steiner is suggesting that scholars should wake up to the depths of Goethe, and regard as serious the places where Goethe has discreetly, lightly, humorously, stated what is actually a very esoteric truth.

[52] The version decided upon by the Archives has here an unconvincing vague sentence, "....someone who could 'begin something' with the words, 'inner', 'higher', 'spiritual self' and so forth."

parts}.[53] There it shows us qualities of this astral complementary form. Thus, we can say to ourselves, because our Higher-self is there, in the realms of the Heavens, thus can we attain an existence in the realms of the Heavens, because here {*on the Earth*} we are able to mould and shape our life.

And now we come to the {*Biblical*} text. I have attempted to translate the Beatitudes in a manner which is in accordance with the meaning of the {*Greek*} words, but also in accordance with the {*real*} meaning of the sentences. You shall see how these translations agree {*with the real meaning of what Christ is revealing*}.[54]

1: *Blessed are the beggars for the Spirit, for in their self is the Kingdom of the Heavens.*

{The usual translation is:*"Blessed are the poor in spirit, for theirs is the Kingdom of Heaven"*}

This {word} "self" is actually there in the Greek ! But above all the {*usual*} phrase, "the spiritually poor" {*or 'the poor of/in spirit'*} is **not there** in the Greek.[55] But rather, "the beggars **for** the Spirit" is there: that is, people who are yearning for the Spirit {*spirituality*}.

> Note:
> We shall translate it in the light of Rudolf Steiner's insights: firstly, precisely correct to the Greek, (so without the 'in'); and then Rudolf Steiner's version as above, (with the 'in'), and then you can see how he has clarified the inner meaning by focussing on the individual 'self' of each 'beggar', rather than all the collective 'beggars for the spirit', with their

---

[53] The manuscript used by the Archives has; "If we give up this spiritual self as the mirror-image in the world of mirror-images, then this shows us the opposites of the polar qualities." This appears to be a defective reading, for it actually has no meaning, and includes the suggestion that a human being would surrender their Higher-self. (!) This passage in the manuscript I have used, contains a deep meaning. The difference arises from just one letter: The official version begins, "Wenn *wir* diese geistige Selbst *aufgeben* {*give up*}..."; my manuscript has, "Dieses geistige Selbst *geht* (*arises*) *uns* als ein Spiegelbild in der Welt der Spiegelungen *auf*"{*for us*}.

[54] This sentence is lacking in the official version.

[55] This sentence is lacking in the official version.

collective many 'selves'. The Greek text can be translated as,

"Blessed are the beggars for the spirit, for of their self is the Kingdom of the Heavens."
(Normally one would say, "for of <u>themselves</u> is the ..." but each person has of course, only one self, so one can indeed say, while still referring to all those people meant by this sentence, "...of their <u>self</u> is the ...).

Rudolf Steiner's accurate, although consciously modified, translation is:

"Blessed are the beggars for the spirit, for in their Self is the Kingdom of the Heavens."

Rudolf Steiner's version is just as correct to the Greek grammar as the usual translations, except where he has added 'in', which more effectively conveys what he knows to be the intended meaning.

(Lecture continues)
Only in the Higher-self does 'the beggar' find the spirit, or the heavenly realms {*whilst living*} on the Earth; and {*this occurs*} after the person has been yearning for the spirit, in the earthly self.

FROM THE NINTH LECTURE, 2nd Dec. 1905:

"Blessed are those who beg for the spirit, for through their own self, they find the Kingdom of the Heavens": this means that in their own self **is** the Kingdom of the Heavens. {*We can note here that in the light of Rudolf Steiner's understanding, we could almost change the word 'beggar' to the artificial word 'begger', that is, one who begs for something, other than money.*}

This is the deep connection between the sensory and the super-sensory world. Whoever strives towards the spirit, they shall find in their self, the complementary form of their striving, that is, the Kingdom of the Heavens. For there is a natural connection between our striving and its mirror-image {counter-part or 'complementary form'}, in the heavenly realms. Nothing could take place in the sensory world which would not have its counter-part in the supersensible. If we

80

despise the spiritual, then the spiritual flees {*from us*}. If we strive for the spirit, then its counter-part streams towards us {*as an occurrence in the astral realm, enhancing our Higher-self*}. In this way did Christ explain these interconnections to the Disciples." Christ Jesus had also spoken in other places of the heavenly realms, or the "kingdom of God". Such a place is in the Gospel of St. Luke, (17:21); but it is usually translated entirely incorrectly.

> (in the NIV it is this):
> Once, having been asked by the Pharisees when the kingdom of God would come, Jesus replied, "The kingdom of God does not come with your careful observation, nor will people say, 'Here it is,' or 'There it is,' because the kingdom of God is within you."

If one translates it according to the meaning, one draws out everything {*that it implies*}, but one does not achieve the real meaning from a dictionary, for this real meaning has to be drawn from an understanding {*arising from*} a deeper expertise. I wish to translate it in this way:

> "When he was questioned by the Pharisees, 'When is the kingdom of God coming"? He answered them; "The kingdom of God does not come {*along with*} the perception" {*that is, the perceiving of what appears to the senses*}. Also, one shall not say, 'Look, over here', or, 'Look, over there', for the kingdom of God is around about us' {*just as is the sensory reality*}." The kingdom of God is around about us, in the same way that the sensory world is.

If we had no eyes, then we would not see any colours and forms {*of objects*}. If we had no ears, we would not hear any sounds. It is the same when those higher, spiritual senses, have opened up; such a person no longer sees only sensory appearances in the environs around him or her, but also the spiritual beings {*which are*} all around us. The spirit which Theosophy teaches, is the same spirit which Christ Jesus taught.[56] So, in essence, Jesus said in his answer,

> Not with the eyes, with which you are able to perceive, and not with the ears, with which you are able to hear, are you able to perceive the kingdom of God, but

---

[56] The Archive book has here used a short sentence from another manuscript: "Christ Jesus taught the spirit."

rather, with the eyes and ears of the spirit; for the kingdom of God is around about you.

Whether we see a spiritual realm of not, depends on whether we possess the organs needed for that kind of perceiving. The same realm we call 'Devachan' is meant by Christ Jesus when he refers to 'Heaven', in the Sermon on the Mount.

Note:
The first difficulty in regard to the passage from St. Luke is about perceiving: whether one translates this as "the perception" as does Rudolf Steiner, or "careful observation" in the NIV, or, as the King James Bible "…it cometh not with observation". This has always puzzled theologians, and Rudolf Steiner's wisdom allows him to point out that the text is simply indicating that physical eyes, or sensory perception, will never reveal the divine reality; because for this one must have clairvoyance.

The more difficult problem arises with the next change Rudolf Steiner has made: instead of *"the kingdom of God is **within** you"*, he has, *"the kingdom of God is **in the midst** of you"; and he expands this by saying it means, "the kingdom of God is **around about us"***. This somewhat vague phrase is accurate to the Greek word here, 'entos' {ἐντος}, and does give a basis for Rudolf Steiner's interpretation, that 'the kingdom of God' is all around us. By contrast to what Rudolf Steiner reveals, theologians normally point out that there are only two possible meanings here. Either, "the Kingdom of God is within you (your soul), or "the Kingdom of God in your midst (among you all)".

Many, but not all, theologians generally reject this second meaning on the grounds that the Kingdom of God can not be said to exist in the Pharisees. What the non-esoteric, theological, viewpoint misses out on here, is a third meaning, which is commonly found in classical Hellenistic Greek texts, and which Rudolf Steiner is using. For this same word also refers to a defined area **around something**, for example it was used by Plato in his *Symposium*, "...he refuses to come *within any distance* {entos - ἐντος} of it." (para.195b).

Rudolf Steiner has pointed to this meaning, in his version: *"the kingdom of God is around about us."* So it means: there is present, behind the material physical world, the spiritual reality, or the Kingdom of God. And this holds true for the Pharisees as well as the followers of Jesus.

In fact, other authentic sayings of Jesus, found in ancient papyrus texts, confirm that Rudolf Steiner is fully correct, in emphasizing that what Christ Jesus really wanted to convey is that 'the kingdom of God' is all around us, but we need clairvoyance to see it. One papyrus records Jesus saying this: 'And the kingdom of God is with you, and also outside of you."[57]

The really clear, and more esoteric version of this saying, preserved for posterity in the *Gospel of St. Thomas*, fully confirms Rudolf Steiner:

His Disciples said to him, "When shall the kingdom {of God} come?" {Jesus answered}, "it will not come by watching for it. Rather, the kingdom of the Father is spread out upon the Earth, but people do not see it.[58]

(Lecture continues)

2 (=3): **"Blessed are the gentle mild-mannered people, for in their self they shall have a share of the Earth."**[59]

{The usual translation is:*"Blessed are the meek, for they will inherit the earth."*}

Through the mild-mannered quality {*existing*} in their earthly self, they shall beget a power in their Higher-self which makes this Earth into their own property. That is to say, these people

---

[57] From Papyrus Oxyrhynchus, 654.9:21.
[58] From the Gospel of St. Thomas, in the *Nag Hammadi Scriptures*, verse 113.
[59] The Archive book has a different text here, "...in their higher self they shall possess the Earth". This appears to be less accurate wording.

shall mould the Earth in the sense of {*imbuing it with*} benevolence and a moral human nature. Not through fury and lower desires of the earthly self, but through gentleness {*existing*} in the earthly self, shall the polar opposite qualities {*to the lower urges*} be brought forth in the Higher-self.[60]

> Note:
> It is intriguing that Rudolf Steiner comments on the 3rd Beatitude, before the 2nd Beatitude in this lecture, yet he does not do this in any of his other lectures.
>
> In fact, this reversal of the 2nd and the 3rd Beatitudes occurs in some early Gospel manuscripts; some as early as the second century. This reversal creates a contrast between the theme of 'beggar' (or poor) and the theme of 'gentle, mild-mannered'.
>
> The old texts which did this, include the significant codex "D", called Bezae Cantabrigiensis, however this is a later document (5th cent), which in most places, (but confusingly, not all places), does not have the authority of earlier texts. Also Clement and Origenes, and various later Church Fathers, reversed the normal sequence.
>
> The contrast this reversal creates, takes the human condition up an ascending ladder, up from poor/beggar to gentle/humble. Scholars have concluded that this is the reason why scribes, when copying the Gospel of St. Matthew, decided to make this change.
>
> But whether Rudolf Steiner here was affirming this idea, or affirming some other veiled idea, is unknown. In any event, it conflicts with the sequence used in his other lectures and therefore with the link of the nine Beatitudes to the nine-fold human being.

FROM THE NINTH LECTURE, 2nd Dec. 1905:

---

[60] The manuscript used by the Archives here adds that, this state of the human being shall "manifest on Earth as a peaceful existence, in a realm of benevolence".

"Those who have not developed in themselves what we call a mild-mannered, gentle disposition, and {*therefore remain*} capable of fury, such people can not 'acquire' for themselves the necessary counter-part, that is, the earthly realm.

{*Note: this sentence is so briefly noted as to be confusing: it means, such people cannot have, as part of themselves, of their spirit, the 'spiritual counterpart', which arises from what a person can acquire as* **an inheritance from many lives** *in the earthly realm.*}

One should not attempt to advance into the heavenly realm, without first redeeming the earthly realm, and only then bringing this {*the result of such spiritualization*} with oneself, into the heavenly realm. We exist on the Earth in order to redeem, to make heavenly, everything which exists on the Earth.

Just as bees fly over the meadows, gathering honey (pollen) from the flowers, and storing it in the bee-hive, so does the soul journey across the world, in order to gather up experiences, and to bring these into the heavenly realms. We need to learn to allow the world to approach us, and to exert is influence in us. Once we have taken up everything into us, when we offer to the world a mild-mannered, gentle disposition and a patient, tolerant quality, then shall the Earth offer something to us.

Note:
There are several implications here. Firstly, the gentle-natured souls are going to 'inherit' the Earth, in the sense that they shall move up and eternally stay with the Earth, as it etherealizes in the future. They shall not fall away into a dismal empty state or place.

Secondly, they shall possess, as a harvest for their soul, that which then accumulates for their spirit, from lifetimes of spiritually striving on Earth.

Thirdly, these souls who have overcome the lower Mars forces, are infusing the Earth – its etheric and astral auras – with high spiritual energies: unless the above words – "these people shall mould the Earth in the sense of {*imbuing it with*} benevolence and a moral human nature" – are not meant to be taken literally. But esoterically, it appears that these words could be viewed literally, as simply an extension of the first implication. That is, the gentle, humble souls shall move up and eternally stay with the Earth, that is, with its ethereal-spiritual nature, in the future, and in becoming an eternal part of the Earth-soul, these souls shall be moulding the planet on a subtle level.

(Lecture continues)
 3 (=2). **"Blessed are those in distress, for in their self they shall find solace."**

{The usual translation is: *Blessed are those who mourn, for they will be comforted.* }

Those who patiently bear their pain, in the normal earthly self, for these people a Higher-self shall arise, in the heavenly realms. This teaching is {*also*} the significant teaching of esotericism; namely that what is 'sown' in the lower person, blossoms forth in the Higher-self.

> Note:
> The commentary here is very brief; we can illuminate this Beatitude further in several aspects. Firstly, the implication of the above commentary is that those who patiently bear their pain are, in fact, making a very fine transformation of their astral body possible. As a result, Rudolf Steiner taught, that whoever bears pain with courage, will have, when they reincarnate, a very fine countenance.
>
> Secondly, the transforming of the soul or astral body assists the development of the Spirit-self. Thirdly, in an archive document, recording a lecture he gave in Rome, Rudolf Steiner explains in regard to this Beatitude, that as the Christ-impulse grows stronger in the human being, ennobling the soul, such a person develops a capacity to heal themselves,
>
> *"The Christ-element even overcomes illnesses, because it {confers the ability to} have mastery over matter. This capacity shall become ever more*

recognized by people, and they shall use it to eradicate illnesses."[61]

(Lecture continues)
4. "Blessed are those who hunger and thirst for righteousness, for they shall be satiated in their Self."

{The usual translation is:"Blessed are those who hunger and thirst for righteousness, for they will be filled.}

Note:
Righteousness, as we noted earlier in this book, is a specifically Biblical term, and really means, an ethical and just, caring social attitude, inspired by moral precepts from God, as given in the Bible. But in this Beatitude, the implication is a social order or society regulated by such ethical, caring and just principles.

(Lecture continues)
Hunger and thirst for 'righteousness' {*in the lower or earthly self*} **is** satiation {*fullness of this*} in the Higher-self.

Just as North and South poles belong together of necessity, so also does the one member {*of the human being*} in the sensory world, belong together with the other member in the spiritual world.

Note:
This sentence "Just as North and South ...." was written by hand onto the typed manuscript page. It was probably written into the page by person who was typing up their transcript about 1905-06, but this is not definite; it may have been added by someone else, years later.[62]

---

[61] Archive lecture, given in Rome at the end of March, 1909.

[62] In the manuscript used by Archives for their book, clarifying words are added here, which come from the author of one of the transcripts, Walter Vegelahn; *"But here one had to add an additional clarifying note: it is not meant that those blessed ones who hunger and thirst for righteousness, shall be satiated in their own self."* However, these words are only necessary if the sentence which occurs in my manuscript, *"Hunger and thirst for 'righteousness' {in the lower or earthly self} is **satiation** {fullness of this} in the Higher-self"*, **are in fact missing** in the Vegelahn transcript – since the

These two sentences imply that later (in this life, or in a future life), 'righteousness' shall accrue in the Higher-self in abundance from the thirst for this, down here.} This is confirmed by the brief words in Chapter Five, from the 1904 lecture, about this Beatitude,

"Such people are craving the spirit, and {*as a consequence*} in their inner being, the heavenly realms are welling forth."

5. "Blessed are the compassionate, because, for them, through their own self, there shall also be compassion."

{The usual Bible translation is:
"Blessed are the merciful, for they will be shown mercy."}

Note:
As the next words from Rudolf Steiner show, the meaning here is that compassion, having been manifested by the person, shall become integrated into the Higher-self. So his translation, given above, can be re-phrased in this way:

"Blessed are the compassionate, because, for them, through their own self, there shall also be compassion – existing in their Higher-self."

(Lecture continues)
When we understand what is meant by the word "compassion', we shall grasp the meaning {*of this Beatitude*} as: the context of the human being.[63] {*That is, the inter-*

___

sentence in the manuscript which I use makes quite clear what is meant. So it appears that this sentence is indeed missing in the manuscript preferred by the Archives, so they were added from the manuscript I used; and yet the above words added by Mr. Vegelahn were still left in the book published by the Archives, even though they were now unnecessary, and thus confusing.

[63] The manuscript used by the Archives here, instead of referring to 'the context', refers to "the harmony" of the human being, and that the human being rays forth this 'harmony'. This appears to be the result of editorial misreading of 'zusammenklang' (harmony), for 'zusammenhang' (context).

connectedness of *the various 'bodies' of the human being: the connection between the soul-body and the devachanic spirit-body or Spiritual-self*}. That is, when we ourselves have an understanding of this context, then shall we ray forth this context {*i.e., this inter-connectedness*} into the higher realms. {*And there, the compassion shall become part of our own Higher-self.*}

6. "Blessed are the pure in heart, for they shall behold God."

{The usual Bible translation is the same: *"Blessed are the pure in heart, for they will see God."*}

This is an especially deep saying, which may be regarded as a foundational maxim of all theosophical and esoteric wisdom. The person who is not pure in heart, that is, a person who has prejudices of an intellectual or moral nature, is a person whose eye, or lenses of the eye, is permeated by false energies. We need to have a pure heart, and in addition to that, also the radiance of a pure heart, if we wish to behold God.

Again we see here the two polarities. Just as the eye can only develop the capacity of sight, if the lenses of the eye are pure {*free of cloudiness or debris*}; just as only an unclouded visual capacity is able to perceive the outer, sensory world, so too, only a pure heart is able to become conscious of God.

FROM THE NINTH LECTURE, 2nd Dec. 1905:
God is unveiled only in the pure heart. The human being who is not in the condition of making his or her heart pure from all that which flows to them from the sense world, can not experience the 'complementary form' {*the astral counter-part*} of this purity in their heart. If the heart is pure, free of sensory 'substance' and memory 'substance', then it can experience God. Whereas that which is full of sensory and memory 'substance', that excludes Divineness. It is {*a question of*} reality and counter-reality: the pure heart – Divinity.[64]

7. "Blessed are the peacemakers, for they shall be become, through themselves, children of God."

---

[64] The text has literally, "of image and counter-image", but this expression is unclear in English.

{The usual translation is:"Blessed are the peacemakers, for they shall be called sons of God."}

(Lecture continues)
In various lectures we have described the lofty future of Christianity. From these, it has become clear that Christianity has very great future power; that it shall become ever greater, more pure and more noble. But, that which this Christianity shall let stream forth into the peoples of the Earth – peace – can only come into existence[65] when, from out of the earthly self, the predisposition for peace {*is developed in the earthly-self and*} surges up towards the Higher-self.

Those people who prepare themselves {*so as to attain*} the predisposition for peace, they shall raise themselves up to the Higher-self, and those who have so raised themselves, shall be called the "children of God".[66]

8. "Blessed are those who are persecuted for righteousness sake, for in their self shall be the Kingdom of Heaven."

{The usual translation is: "Blessed are those who are persecuted because of righteousness, for theirs is the Kingdom of Heaven."}

Persecution means {*needing a*} refuge. {*The condition of being subject to persecution because of a profound inner spirituality means, one needs a refuge.*} This dynamic is a mirror-imaging situation {*between the physical world and the astral realm*}. For if I am persecuted today, in my earthly self, then I find refuge in the Higher-self: that is the other polarity.

---

[65] The manuscript used by the Archives states, that "this peace can only become **God**, when...": but this is without any real meaning, compared to the wording in the manuscript I have used: "this peace can only come **into existence**, when..."

[66] Note: the NINTH LECTURE, 2nd Dec. 1905, commentary here actually has a segment which is not related to the Beatitudes as such, but which is related to the Freemasonry theme of Cain and Abel. It states that the 'children of God' are the Abel type of person, (priests/ mystics); the 'children of human beings' are the Cain type (engage in earthly deeds and knowledge), and then, unexpectedly, the notes next mention that "the Jesuits seek to dull people down". This dulling down consists of not letting people experience the Cain life of earthly engagement. These brief notes probably excluded some connecting comments, thereby making his words here appear odd.

{And in the Higher-self shall be the Kingdom of the Heavens. That is, high spiritual-devachanic being-ness; a beginning of the Life-spirit.}[67]

In this way we are to read these noble words, in the theosophical sense. It is necessary today to emphasize this core part of the Sermon on the Mount, because we live in a time where again a core of humanity must be made aware of this Higher-self, of the Kingdom of the Heavens, in order that they can consciously strive towards this.

A core group of humanity must again become true, genuine Christians. Overcoming of the separated-state is a truth: *{it is}* attaining the Higher-self....the future can only bring about *{a}* spiritualized humanity, if the entirely free, pure, Christian spirit is re-discovered. We need *{to be inspired by}* the original Primal Power. The Higher-self has to arise out of an original, Primal Reality.

> **Note:**
> The expression the "original, Primal Power/Reality" appears to refer to the divine source of creation, including the human spirit. This is what Rudolf Steiner refers to as 'the Cosmos Spirit'; this means in effect, the great divinities in the sun sphere: the Elohim, and in particular, the cosmic Christ.

FROM THE NINTH LECTURE, 2nd Dec. 1905:
Here we see the contrast to that which was proclaimed in the First Beatitude: the begging for the spirit proceeds from out of the human being itself. Now *{in this Beatitude}* we encounter that which is exerting an influence from outside of the human being – here, in this Beatitude, *{it is implied that}* a mirroring dynamic forms *{"...for in their self shall be the Kingdom of Heaven". That is, a person at this high level, is an embodiment of the Spirit.}*

So the dynamic of this Beatitude proceeds in a counter direction to that of the first Beatitude *{for in this, the self does not have any spiritual content, but is seeking it, so, as a consequence or response in the astral realm, the spirit draws near to that person's soul}*.

---

[67] Some "of the Life-spirit or Buddhi shall be in their self", lecture: 15th March 1910, in GA 118.

It becomes ever clearer to us that such a countering or mirroring dynamic is a primary feature of the Sermon on the Mount. Through realizing this, we gain a deeper understanding of what Jesus gave to his Disciples "on the mountain", that is, in the Mystery place.

(Lecture from 1905 continues)
Consider for a moment what has occurred in our history. Normally one does not consider at all deeply enough the pages of world history. Starting in earlier times, the world of materialism has gradually become prominent: this is appropriate, for all that has happened in history is necessary {*for humanity's evolving*}. Through this world of materialism, an intellectual orientation has come about which is limited to simply the sense world.

This mindset is actually the 'spirit' of materialism; but materialism no longer has any {*evolutionary*} importance for humanity. For people of insight, materialism is already now superstition and worship of idols {*its task is over*}. If we view our situation in this way, then we shall see that, in a certain sense, the feeling for the spirit is already present; the spirit which is now to be poured out {*for humanity*}....

> Note:
> Here references to the Beatitudes cease. This 1905 lecture does not have any reference to the ninth Beatitude. The last section of this lecture is about the social and economic challenges of society; this section is given in Appendix 3.
>
> That materialism is described as no longer relevant, as a mind-set whose time has passed, is quite striking. In the century or more since this lecture was given, materialism has obviously deepened its grip on humanity, and gained much more social authority. Rudolf Steiner would have known that this was very likely to happen, but nevertheless wished to communicate to his audience that it is a fact that an underlying dynamic exists, enhanced from the spiritual worlds, which seeks to enable the re-emergence of a spiritual worldview, and of higher consciousness.
>
> This dynamic is associated with a new tendency affecting the lives of human beings. This is, upon

incarnating, not to merge so deeply into their body –
reversing a tendency which began some millennia
ago, and which intensified as from the 4th century
AD. The result of this is that a slightly psychic
condition has arisen, which leads to a sensitivity to
the ethers.

Chapter Seven

Concluding insights into the Beatitudes

1: (contemplating the physical body)

Blessed are the beggars for the spirit, for they shall find in their self the kingdoms of Heaven.

The essence of the revelations from Rudolf Steiner about this Beatitude is, in general terms, that through the entry into the Earth's aura of the cosmic Christ, the mighty leader of the Powers, those human beings who have a capacity for spiritual awareness, are able to undertake spiritual development, despite the density of the physical body. Consequently the spiritual seeker feels that their own nature is incomplete unless he or she develops their spiritual potential, so they become 'beggars' as to the spirit.

Here we need to look again at the last sentence in source 'B' for this Beatitude:

> Blessed those people can be, who are beggars for the spirit, who no longer receive the spirit as a gift from outside, in accordance with old way of perceiving. Blessed can they be, when they take into themselves the Christ-impulse – for then through the development of their I , they themselves can **become** the Kingdoms of Heaven !

This remarkable sentence is saying that this person, their "I" or Self, can blossom into the Spiritual-self – which is a manifestation of the spiritual worlds – but this only happens as people seek to spiritualize themselves, and that this is a process which is connected to the assistance that the Christ subtly offers.

  The further implications are that through the Christ-light in the Earth, the "I" or self-sense of such people, has within it a capacity to attain spirituality – but that this capacity is due to the existence in the human soul of the Christ-light, in a germinal form. But how is this possible ? It is a deep conviction of Christian people that Christ offers the opportunity for spirituality, to receive the 'Divine' into one's soul. But since esoteric truths were not to be included in

Christian theology, the deeper secrets of a process which changes the aura or soul of the person, allowing the Spirit-self to arise, as a result of an active inner life, has never really been clearly known.

There are several answers to this deep question from anthroposophy. One is that since the cosmic Christ-light pervades the Earth's aura, any true spiritual seeking shall naturally have an inner assistance give to them. This is what is meant by the words of Jesus in St. John's Gospel (14:16, 26, & 15:26, 16:7) that, he shall send the Holy Spirit or Helper (Paraclete) to human beings.

But we can also briefly note that a study of Rudolf Steiner's words about the mission of the mysterious Archangel Vidar, mentioned in the Edda, reveals another process which helps the spiritual rebirth of the human being. Although the Edda derives from ancient Druidic spiritual knowledge, the various beings mentioned in that book are not relevant only to the Nordic world, they have, like the Greek and Indian gods, a mission for the Earth in general. The essence of what is indicated about this Archangel is, that it assists the intentions of Christ, by bringing about the sacred process of the 'Virgin Birth' in each soul. This esoteric phrase refers to a process which involves giving to each incarnating soul, prior to birth, a germinal form of the Spirit-self.

This potential, which is similar to the exquisite spiritual purity and goodness naturally in the infant and toddler, can be enlivened by the attempts towards spirituality by the adult, to eventually blossom powerfully.[68] This process is then like a shimmering white lily-bud being placed within the darkened red tones of the soul, coursing through the blood. (This archangelic activity is explained in my book *The Vidar Flame column – its meaning from Rudolf Steiner.*)

There is a further way to understand the implication that the Christ-Light can so help the self to spiritualize itself, to enable a person to seek spirituality even in our times, when living more closely embedded in the body, which itself is denser than in previous millennia. This possibility is clearer when we know of the dynamics that have existed between the sun-gods (hence the Christ) and humanity, throughout earlier evolutionary Ages, as revealed in Rudolf Steiner's *An Outline of Esoteric Science.*

In the long ages of our evolution, prior to the Earth existing as a planet cast out of the sun, an influence was exerted by solar deities, led by the cosmic Christ, on the human soul

---

[68] This sacred theme is explained in my *The Vidar Flame Column – its meaning from Rudolf Steiner.*

from the cosmos, and this influence has been present ever since. It was awareness of this dynamic amongst the initiated priests and priestesses of ancient cultures, that resulted in a universal 'sun-worship'. When the Earth was cast out of the sun, in a remote epoch, this was not only a physical, molecular event; it included the etheric forces and hosts of astral beings who now form the Earth's soul.

As the earth cooled and condensed into the relatively stable and solid planet of today, people began the long and arduous journey of lifetimes on a planet which was at first, a substantially aquatic planet, which gradually cooled, but which was still subject to violent volcanic activity. Over long time-cycles, the sun-gods ensured that their influences rayed down into the primitive astral nature of humanity, moderating the self-seeking or destructive influences from Luciferic and Ahrimanic beings. So we have been, and are, powerfully influenced by, and deeply interconnected with, the sun gods or the 'Elohim'.

This spiritual perspective on evolution helps us to see the reality of what underlies the words of the cosmic Christ in this Beatitude; namely that human beings, if they so wish, can develop an awareness of the spiritual world, despite a deeper immersion in a denser body. These words are in effect declaring that the influence of the cosmic Christ on humanity, once this great deity has merged with the Earth's aura, shall continue to be exerted.

Rudolf Steiner's commentary on this Beatitude teaches that the influence of this great Being on the human "I" or self-consciousness, is such that the deeper immersion of the soul in the body in recent times, does not prevent an interest in spiritual development. In effect, he is saying that an intuitive or holistic awareness can still arise today; and this means, in terms of anthroposophical psychology, that the spiritual-soul can be empowered, and eventually blossom into the Spiritual-self.

But there is another possibility here, and this is the impact of the Christ-light on the body itself. In my book, *Rudolf Steiner on Leonardo's Last Supper*, an archive document is provided wherein Rudolf Steiner explains that a replica of the physical body of Jesus – the archetype of humanity's redeemed physical body of the future, (not the flesh substances) – is available for human beings to absorb. This is at first a startling idea, but it is really only an extension of the well-known idea that the soul of a spiritual seeker can absorb spiritual light from the Christ (which is in effect, divine goodness and wisdom.)

It is possible that this Beatitude is affirming the deep mystery of the process which is intended to transform the physical body, to help protect it from a subtle inner hardening. This is pointing to an activity from Christ which extends the concept of 'Salvation' beyond what is usually understood by this term: to the physical body also (but not its flesh or material aspect).[69]

The dynamic of ennobling the soul by transforming the lower Mars forces, is interconnected with the condition of the physical body. Lowly Mars actions often manifest in the soul via the organs of the physical-flesh body; a process which can degrade the underlying energetic template of the body.[70] So a 'beggar for the spirit', that is someone who really wants to undertake spiritual development, is also helping to ennoble their body.[71] A brief remark preserved from Origenes appears to refer to this interconnected dynamic,

> The Earth is the exalted inheritance of the 'Living Ones', hence these souls are inheritors of their own glorified and incorruptible bodies.[72]

The phrase, the 'Living Ones', appears to refer to those human beings who have received new life from the Christ-impulse.

The first Beatitude is saying that, as from the time of Golgotha, but especially as from the modern era, if souls strongly seek ('beg') to develop spiritually, then this seeking shall be strengthened by the Christ-forces, now present in the Earth, and hence several results occur:

1: in the germinal Higher-self of such a person, spiritual influences are emerging into being, despite the denser bodily reality

2: progress in their spiritual quest is therefore more likely

---

[69] A strange phenomenon exists, which may point to this mystery; the incorruptible bodies of various Christian saints.

[70] This subtle, invisible template of the body was called 'the phantom' by Rudolf Steiner, meaning a tenuous, spectral energy-form.

[71] Rudolf Steiner in fact revealed (lecture 18th Dec. 1912) that the inherently low, animalistic qualities in the Mars sphere are a specific focus for initiates in the Christ-Mysteries; a specific work is being undertaken to improve the Mars forces by the 'Beloved Disciple' and the most recent Buddha, Gautama Siddhartha.

[72] Origenes, from the catenae, (Γῆ ἐστι κληρονομία ἡ ὑψηλὴ τῶν Ζώντων....) in Klostermann (ref. 9) p. 49.

3: If such an impulse is present in a person, especially in the times when a natural holistic-psychic sensing has faded away, then in that person's "I", a higher spiritual presence exists. The Spiritual-self is announcing itself to them; it is exerting its influence in their soul – and this is the result of the influence emanating from the Christ, as the indwelling Spirit of the Earth. (This is what is meant by the old term, the 'Holy Spirit'.)

Beatitude 2: (contemplating the etheric body)
   "Blessed are those who take pain and sorrow upon themselves, for through their self, they shall be comforted."

Rudolf Steiner's commentaries view this saying from different perspectives; some refer to soul distress and others to physical pain, some to both things. It emerges from these commentaries that there are three aspects to this Beatitude. It is significant that source 'B' states that the Beatitude refers to those who **consciously seek** to deal with their pain.

Firstly, in regard to a spiritually striving person who is seeking to overcome the general distress felt in the soul from a heightened awareness of their lower self, Christ is proclaiming in this Beatitude that people can achieve their goal of purity through the presence of the Christ-forces in the Earth-soul (which is formed from all the beings and energies that constitute the etheric, astral and devachanic auras of the Earth.) But this Beatitude is about the impact of the Christ impulse on the etheric body, so the implication here is that the distress refers to lower impulses of the soul which are more deep-seated, more difficult to conquer, because they are habitual or in one's predisposition.

But any impulse which is habitual, or pre-dispositional, has taken hold of one's life-forces or etheric body. The energy sustaining these lower impulses can be conquered through the Christ-energy permeating the Earth's ethers. From there, a purifying life-force can ray into the etheric body of a spiritual seeker.[73] Underlying this Beatitude is the veiled subject of the removal from the etheric body of malignant elemental energies, if the soul turns strongly towards the Christ-impulse.

In regard to this theme, a precious esoteric text from the Hellenistic era has survived, which comes from initiation wisdom, and is about the existence in the Earth of various etheric streams, which are imbued with noble energies, associated with the sun-sphere. This text is a hymn to Apollo, who in Greek mythology represents the sun-god. Such worship of Apollo and other sun-beings originate in pre-Christian times; but Rudolf Steiner explains that Apollo is a representative of what we now can call the cosmic Christ. As I mentioned in *The Hellenistic Mysteries and Christianity*, Rudolf Steiner describes Apollo as a kind of representative of Christ or Osiris. He seeks to help people to attain to spirituality, and the Muses are his assistants. He can be regarded as a symbol of the sun god – the great central deity of antiquity. My translation of this hymn, which is very complex in its Greek structure, reads,

The Hymn to Apollo:

And so for Thee {Apollo}, springs of flowing spiritual-intelligence well forth,
located within caves, nurturing the Earth by
the divine inspiration of the Muse's oracular utterance:
itself proceeding from a divine voice.
And these spiritual energies break through
beyond the earth's surface,
by flowing everywhere,
thus conferring on mortals
the perpetual outpourings of sweet streams.

The hymn is making the remarkable assertion that, for the sake of Apollo, which means owing to the influence of Apollo, and what this deity would like humanity to spiritually achieve, there actually exists in the Earth-sphere, ethereal streams or

---

[73] Behind this mystery is veiled the theme of lowly elemental beings or energies becoming replaced with wholesome energies.

currents of energy which are permeated by a spiritual intelligence (or 'astrality'). In this Apollonian hymn, the word 'caves' appears to refer to the Earth's mineral crust, pictured as a subterranean realm. And this crust of the Earth is viewed as permeated by currents of certain subtle energies. These subtle streams of ethereal energies are said to nurture material substance from out of the ether.

So the uplifting and reverential message from the Apollo priesthood is: matter is not the only factor here on Earth, in which we live, move and have our being, for there are spiritual energies here, too, and they can help to release our incarnate consciousness from the grip of matter. These currents of spiritual energies, inwardly resonating to distant celestial tones, surge along, passing through mineral substances and then permeate human beings.

And in doing this they are giving to sensitive people an awareness of spiritual realities, or at of least higher truths. In the symbolic language of the hymn, they surge upwards beyond the surface of the Earth, and into people. Their influence is described as delightful or sweet, indicating their uplifting and spiritualizing nature. The Beatitude appears to be referring to such etheric streams of energy, which are now permeated by the cosmic Christ, who is no longer active from the remote sun sphere, but indwelling in the planet's aura.

Secondly, Rudolf Steiner's explanations of this Beatitude is teaching that the human being who is striving to deal with physical suffering, derived from illness, can now, through the influence of the Christ-impulse active in the etheric body, be moved towards ways of reducing illness and its associated suffering; or even of being healed.

The message here is that the presence of Christ has imbued the human etheric body with new powers to bring about its healing. Historically, it is the case that many Christian saints have been credited with healing powers, a blessed dynamic which was inaugurated through Jesus, and then bestowed upon the Disciples. Such a healing process can imply that the sufferer is enabled to approach their illness as the result of a soul imbalance (possibly, but not necessarily, with a karmic origin), and to thereby invoke a restoration of a healthy condition.

Thirdly, the human being who is striving to deal with physical pain as such (not caused by illness), there is likewise, through the influence of the Christ-impulse active in the etheric body, a capacity now given to humanity to find the inner strength to more capably withstand suffering. There is also the implication in the commentaries, that human beings do need to encounter pain, and hence it is of value to one's inner life, to try to prevent the pain dominating fully.

In this context, Rudolf Steiner mentions that Christ wished to inform people in this situation that, as evolution moves onwards, it would soon cease to be viable to seek to bring about a strange, ecstatic body-free state, to avoid feeling pain. The number of people in an ancient culture who could carry out this odd practice was in any event, presumably limited.

The powerful comments of Rudolf Steiner, found in an archive document, from a lecture he gave in Rome, which I have included in an earlier chapter, is crucial here; namely,

> The Christ-element even overcomes illnesses, because it {confers the ability to} have mastery over matter. This capacity shall become ever more recognized by people, and they shall use it to eradicate illnesses.

It is widely accepted that some reports from earlier centuries of Christian saints curing people of severe illnesses are genuine. Here, Rudolf Steiner is indicating that people in any century, if they pursue the path to high spirituality, can imbue their etheric body with higher etheric forces, drawn from the cosmic Christ, now existing in our planet's aura, and develop healing powers.

(There can be a similar healing capacity, wherever priests or priestesses have a capacity for healing bestowed upon them from beings in the spiritual world. An alternative condition that has allowed people to be healers occurs when there is an unusual condition of the etheric body; if this extends beyond the physical body more than usual, then the out-raying etheric energies naturally would have a tendency restore any damage or disease in the body.)

The second Beatitude is saying, as from the time of Golgotha, but especially as from the modern era that:

1: Those who are genuinely on the spiritual path and become troubled by their lower urges shall find that an inner helper is available from the Holy Spirit or Paraclete. These influences can help triumph over these imperfections, including, it seems, those which have become ingrained (absorbed into the etheric body, from the aura or soul-body).

2: Those who are struggling with the suffering caused by illness are now offered a source of healing, from etheric energies raying out from Christ.

3: Those who were struggling with physical pain and induced an ecstatic body-free psychic state to cope, and also modern people who can use medication to block out pain, should endeavour to develop the inner strength to endure their pain – to some extent. The commentaries are not specific about the Christ-influence in terms of pain, but the implication is that some soul-comforting is available, and also that enduring discomfort has a strengthening, ennobling effect upon the "I".

Beatitude 3: (contemplating the astral body)
  Blessed are those who are of a gentle and calm predisposition, for they shall inherit the Earth.

When in remote times, the germinal human being received a soul, or soul-body, in an earlier evolutionary Age, this aura glowing around their physical-etheric had only a primitive, animalistic quality.[74] The beings who bestowed this were the 'Mights' in the language of St. Paul; Rudolf Steiner reveals that from these high beings, the Spirits of Movement, all the animal group-souls derive. In our current Aeon, it was in the Lemurian epoch that we humans emerged as primitive beings. This is described by Rudolf Steiner in his *An Outline of Esoteric Science.*

Consequently today, our astral nature contains, in its deeper levels, some very unpleasant animal-like qualities (depending upon how much we have evolved ourselves). If by the end of the Earth phase of our existence, we have become calm and gentle, devoid of fury and lusts, then we shall have conquered these lower energies. But this is a very real battle, and as Rudolf Steiner reveals, there shall be some souls who may not succeed, and in them the animal urges could re-emerge strongly.

This truth was known to ancient Egyptians, and other initiates; the sphinx is the image that they created to visualize this dynamic. (Not the Sphinx near the Great Pyramid, which is that of a lion and a human head, but the kind of sphinx

---

[74] This earlier vast epoch is called the 'Moon Aeon'.

102

that was often depicted in Mesopotamian art, with bull, eagle, lion and human parts.)

The third Beatitude is saying that those souls who endeavour to conquer the lowly, primitive 'astrality' or 'soul qualities' – most of which derive from Mars – and succeed in attaining a gentle, humble, balanced, soul nature, shall have gained the treasure of what our lifetimes on the Earth offer.

Beatitude 4: (contemplating the sentient-soul)

> **"Blessed are those who strive for righteousness, for they shall be satiated in themselves."** (mss. 1905)

(or)

> **"Blessed are those who feel a hunger and thirst for righteousness, for this yearning shall be appeased through their own self."**

Contemplations on the fourth Beatitude:
The implication of Rudolf Steiner's commentaries is that in the emotions of those people who are yearning for righteousness, that is, yearning for a prevailing of good-will and fairness in society, there exists an enhanced source of these qualities. This source is the effect of the Christ-light. In addition, we noted earlier (page 43) that Rudolf Steiner also taught that this process is to occur for a purpose:

> **namely, that these people in possessing this 'righteousness' through its presence in them, cancel out the un-righteousness** existing in the world (that is, in the wider social group to which these people belong).

It is this statement which reflects precisely how our feelings or emotions function: they diffuse themselves out into other people in a veiled manner. Whereas a concept often has to be explained for someone else to grasp it. But our feelings, which extend into the semi-conscious sphere of our soul-life, subtly flow into the soul-life of other people. For example, we all know how, if we are amongst a group of people who are feeling very depressed, or fearful, or in some state of hilarious laughter, we ourselves can take on these very feelings – despite having no intention of doing this.

We see here how this Beatitude is correlated to the sentient-soul or emotional life, and not the intellectual-soul. We also can see clearly how the intellectual-soul is much more an expression of the "I" than the sentient-soul.

Beatitude 5: (contemplating the intellectual-soul)
"Blessed are the compassionate(-merciful), for through themselves, they shall receive compassion."

It is helpful now, if we consider again these two extracts from Rudolf Steiner's commentaries,

> What is developed in the intellectual-soul, once this has developed the Christ-quality, this must be, above all else, a *human* quality.

> ....the human being, when he or she absorbs the Christ-power, can develop those virtues which flow from one being to another being of the same kind {*namely, human beings*}.

He taught that this Beatitude refers to our logical thinking capacity, or 'intellectual-soul'; but in the various members of the human being, this represents the ego or "I"; that is, our sense of self. As we contemplate compassion, or being compassionate, it becomes clear, especially in difficult circumstances, that the individual self really does have to make an inner effort to consciously triumph over anger, resentment, and giving priority to one's own wishes, or indifference to others.

We saw earlier that the Greek word in this Beatitude (eleeo) can mean either compassion or mercy, and that mercy is a more intense, more demanding form of giving compassion. For the ancient Greeks did have a specific verb for compassion (splagchnizomai – σπλαγχνίζομαι), as distinct from 'mercy'.

But the situation in the Gospels is unusual, in that the specific verb for compassion is reserved in the New Testament for exceptional and intense emotions, usually felt by Jesus, just before he carries out miraculous healings.[75] So

---

[75] In the Septuagint, from about 300 BC, the sentence occurs, "the one who is compassionate, shall be shown mercy". Here the two different verbs are clearly used. (This phrase, although less significant than the Beatitude, is

the other verb (eleeo), which is translated as 'compassion' in the Beatitude, also means 'mercy'. So we also need clarity about the nature of mercy, as an expression of the self, of the self-conscious ego.

In a play by William Shakespeare, there is a speech which conveys what is implied by Rudolf Steiner's commentaries on this Beatitude. It is the speech by Portia, in *The Merchant of Venice* (Act 4: sc1). When this is carefully studied, with awareness that initiatory spiritual wisdom has been interwoven into many parts of Shakespeare's plays (and his sonnets), we can uncover some deep truths.

The speech by Portia is designed to persuade the merchant, Shylock, not to proceed with his lawsuit of demanding a pound of flesh. It is a magnificent presentation of why mercy should be given by a person who has a position of power and authority. The specific interaction in this scene between the various characters is not the point of interest here, but rather the way that mercy itself is described, because this is relevant to the Beatitude.

Following is the main part of the speech by Portia, firstly in a version with some discreet modernizing of the language, and then in the 400 year-old original text. I provide this slightly modernized version first, because in my experience, and study of Shakespeare, the meaning of many speeches in his plays is lost to people, because the now archaic language is no longer understood in places:

Portia:
> The quality of mercy is not exaggerated.
> It droppeth as the gentle rain from heaven
> Upon the place beneath. It is twice blest:
> It blesseth him that gives and he that takes.
> 'Tis mightiest in the mightiest; it honours
> The thronèd monarch more than does his crown.
> His scepter shows the force of temporal power:
> The symbol that inspires awe and majesty
> Wherein doth sit the dread and fear of kings;
> But mercy is above this scept'red sway.
> It is enthronèd in the hearts of kings;
> It is an attribute of God Himself;
> And earthly power doth then appear likest God's
> When mercy moderates justice....

---

similar, to some extent; it was added to the Proverbs in the Septuagint without any explanation, and is thus of unknown origin.)

This speech in its original, superb English, has quite a number of terms which are now archaic. Also the rules of English grammar were still being established in Elizabethan times; hence a Shakespearean sentence or phrase can be literally incorrect to our grammar today, and therefore very confusing. The words in italics in the original version below, indicate those which have been modernized, above.

> The quality of mercy is not *strained*.
> It droppeth as the gentle rain from heaven
> Upon the place beneath. It is twice blest:
> It blesseth him that gives and *him* that takes.
> 'Tis mightiest in the mightiest; it *becomes*[76]
> The thronèd monarch *better* than his crown.
> His scepter shows the force of temporal power,
> The *attribute*[77] *to* awe and majesty
> Wherein doth sit the dread and fear of kings;
> But mercy is above this sceptered sway.
> It is enthronèd in the hearts of kings;
> It is an attribute *to*[78] God Himself;
> And earthly power doth then *show* likest God's
> When mercy *seasons* justice.....

This speech is telling us that being merciful to a person whom one is fully allowed to severely punish (the merchant, Shylock), requires a consciously ethical decision. Such a decision can only arise when the "I" engages strongly with the situation that it finds itself in. The natural feeling is to be avenged, or to enforce laws without flexibility, or to reinforce one's authority: these have to be dismissed, and replaced with a kindness, arising from an empathy for the plight of the guilty person, or an awareness of the many benefits to society that the demonstration of compassion brings about.

Furthermore, the speech tells us that the person being merciful becomes blessed through such a non-egoistical, highly ethical, action. This sentence in the speech directly echoes the Beatitude. And it is a statement which is literally true, as higher spiritual energies do light up in the aura of a person who acts in an ethical manner, and can create a

---

[76] As D. & B. Crystal point out in *Shakespeare's Words: a Glossary*", 'becoming' in Shakespeare's works can mean 'of pleasing appearance', but not here; it means 'to honour', as also in King Edward III.

[77] 'Attribute' here is understood to mean a symbol, not a characteristic feature; this usage by Shakespeare is specified in the full Oxford English Dictionary (meaning #3).

[78] These words mean either: 'an attribute *of* God', (as the use of dative and possessive cases were not yet fixed) or 'an *ascription* to God (of that quality)'.

momentum that carries that person to a higher level of humanity.

But, says Portia, the recipient of the mercy is also blessed: this also is literally true, as the effect of receiving mercy in a dire situation exposes the recipient to a potent example of compassion, and this often induces in that person a determination to be compassionate themselves; to be merciful to others, including – should the situation ever be reversed – to the one who was earlier merciful to oneself.

As Portia's speech indicates, the effect of a ruler or a person in authority showing mercy, is often that the people around them become especially loyal and respectful. The quality of mercy they have demonstrated then becomes their 'mightiest' aspect, and it also bestows more honour on an authority than the symbols of their authority. Such a ruler does become a greater reality than "his crown" – the glow of an illusory 'majesty' which old aristocratic lineages exert on the popular mind.

Hence "blessed are the merciful, for they shall receive mercy": the implementing of compassion or mercy in society causes this quality to spread, and become the norm in society. Eventually those who bestow mercy or compassion as a new, or newly affirmed, social way of being, may themselves receive a compassionate response from their community, when the need arises.

Perhaps the reason that mercy (and compassion) are so honoured, is that people have not only a feeling for the ethical achievement that a merciful individual has attained, but also awareness that it is an expression of a truly ethical deed arising from within that person, and not in response to external cultural expectations.[79]

This dynamic closely affirms the teaching of Rudolf Steiner, that the purpose of the Earth itself – that is of human beings having repeated incarnations in a physical body – is to bring into existence the capacity for Love. He explains that the environment around us is permeated with wisdom (the 'laws of Nature') which derive from the Gods, as they created the Earth in its previous cosmic phase (the Moon Aeon). The new Earth in its next cosmic existence, is meant to be permeated by Love, **which is to derive from human beings**; from people who have achieved the spiritualizing of their "I".

As we noted earlier, in his lectures on this Beatitude given in later years, he emphasizes that, because the normal,

---

[79] We don't have space here to comment on the subtle message in the play, about how the victorious nominal Christians display an appalling lack of 'mercy' to the defeated Shylock

earthly-self has consciously manifested compassion to others, this results in other people being compassionate to him or her. From this social dynamic, the planet itself can be permeated by these forces of compassion and love.

Beatitude 6: (contemplating the spiritual-soul)
"Blessed are those who have purity in their hearts, for through themselves, they shall behold God."

The usual translations of the Sixth Beatitude, which declare that spiritualized people shall "see God", are inadequate, if one is seeking to understand more clearly, more esoterically what it is saying. As given earlier, my translation is: "Blessed are those pure as to the heart, for they shall spiritually perceive divine being-ness."

The idea that people shall 'see' any non-physical reality has to be referring to clairvoyance; and perception of 'God' – if this word refers to the ultimate, unknowable First Cause – is unlikely to be meant (see below).

Rudolf Steiner's translation is not really different from what my careful translation presents. But he goes beyond the actual Greek, to emphasize that the Saviour wishes to communicate here, that this achievement shall be the result of the "I" of the person undertaking the inner effort needed to develop a highly purified, chaste soul.

He retains the verb 'to see' and the noun 'God', probably to keep within the traditional language, and to avoid further complex explanations; he just comments that such translations are not so good. (Elsewhere he comments that the term 'God' is an abstraction, and actually refers to the influence of the ranks of divine-spiritual beings.)

I have used the phrase "spiritually perceive" because this is much more correct than 'to see', for the Greek verb here (horaoe - ὁράω), was **almost never used for physical seeing**. Instead, it had a major role in Greek literature for clairvoyant perception, for discerning spirits and deities. And it is this kind of 'seeing' that is meant, since 'God' is not a material being.

We can replace the word 'God' with 'divine being-ness'; there are several reasons for this. The Greek word used is 'theos' (θεος), which certainly does have the meaning, 'God', but it also has other meanings. The idea of 'God' is engulfed in much confusion due to its abstract nature; different ancient writers and religions, meant different beings when they used this word.

Furthermore, its usage by Jesus was, as Rudolf Steiner explains, designed in part, to give to Christians the idea of a great, single Creator, from whom their soul derives. But such an educative process had, by sheer necessity, to lead to simplistic, confused, and often superficial interpretations, especially as the Christian world was soon to lose knowledge of the nine ranks of Hierarchical beings which mediate between humans and a 'First Cause' or ultimate God.

However, any insightful person knows that perception of an ultimate 'First Cause' or Primal Godhead, a being beyond even the highest of the nine ranks of divine beings involved in creation, the sublime Seraphim, is virtually impossible – so the word 'God' is meant to point the Christian towards some lesser, but still holy, spiritual reality. Indeed Moses himself, a high Initiate (having passed through the awesome ancient Egyptian Mysteries) could obtain only a distant glimpse of Jehovah.

He had asked to clairvoyantly behold the glory of God (that is, Jehovah), but was informed, as related in the Book of Exodus (33:21-23), that he could only glimpse a narrow view of the 'back' of God (that is, his indirect reflection), not of his direct manifestation ('face'). Yet Jehovah, though a great deity, is not the final supreme Godhead.

We discover the answer to what is meant by this Beatitude when we know that firstly this same word, *theos*, also means any deity or 'god'.[80] It has meant this from the ancient Greek of Homer (about 750 BC), through to the Hellenistic Age with Plato, etc, and on into the time of Jesus, and beyond.

But secondly, and very important, throughout this same time-frame, *theos* also meant 'divine-ness' or 'divine being-ness'. For example, Bishop Ignatius wrote (in about AD 110) that the congregation at Magnesia should strive to work together, in 'divine unity of intention' or in 'godly harmony' (*hen homonoia theou* - ἐν ὁμονοίᾳ θεοῦ); here he has used the word *theos* to mean 'divine/godly'.

So, in the Beatitude, the meaning is that, as the Spirit-self arises in the now chaste, sanctified soul, (a person with a purified heart), a higher consciousness shall start to develop, and as a result, the acolyte begins to perceive – with their clairvoyance or higher faculties of perception – glimpses of a 'divine being-ness'. This divine reality which is perceived, is

---

[80] So, for my readers who know ancient Greek, the phrases 'the *Theos*' (τον Θεον, του Θου, τῷ Θεω) were used for various deities and for 'divine being-ness', not only for a supreme Being.

the divine nature of the acolyte's own Spirit-self: not of a theoretically conjectured ultimate Godhead.

My interpretation is affirmed in the esoteric initiation wisdom of the ancient world, in the writings known as the Hermetic Texts. These texts contain mystical-esoteric wisdom derived from the ancient Egyptian Mysteries, which were preserved for posterity after being translated into Greek, in the Hellenistic Age.

In Book 13 of *The Hermetica,* (paragraph 14), there occurs a passage which is drawn from the same initiatory perspective embedded in the sixth Beatitude. An acolyte on the pathway to initiation is in dialogue with a source of wisdom, named as "Hermes", who was the great initiate responsible for the blossoming of a high spiritual culture in Egypt around 2,900 BC. The acolyte has now advanced considerably, and so Hermes says to him,

> Do you not know that by a process, natural to the spirit, you have grown into a divine being, {*theos*} and thus a child of The One, as I am? [81]

These words of Hermes could be compressed as,

"Do you not know that you have become divine (a god)...",

This is the meaning of the words of Jesus, "Do you not know that you are (*can become*) gods?" [82] And it appears that exactly this is the meaning of the Beatitude: to 'spiritually perceive divine being-ness' or godliness, in oneself, that is, in one's dawning higher "I". Hence the Beatitude is saying:

> "Blessed are those pure as the heart, for they shall spiritually perceive divine being-ness {in themselves, but deriving from higher beings.}"

Beatitude 7: (contemplating the Spiritual-self)
"Blessed are those who establish peace, for through themselves, they shall become children of God."

It is important here to note that, in the deepest Gospel, the Gospel of St. John, when the Risen Saviour first appeared to

---

[81] In the Greek text, ἀνοεῖς ὅτι θεὸς πέθυκας, καὶ τοῦ ἑνὸς παῖς, ὁ κἀγώ; the word πέθυκας (pethukas) contains the meaning of a natural process through which something grows or comes up.

[82] See the Appendix 4 for a note about the words of Jesus, "you are gods".

the Disciples, to their etheric perception, he said (John 20:19), "Peace unto you".[83] Then this Gospel records that soon thereafter, on the next two occasions, when Jesus was perceived by the Disciples, these words were spoken again as a kind of greeting. This was not meant as a normal earthly greeting, but as words of power, a blessing, through which the Saviour was helping the Disciples to attain to a higher spirituality, to their Spirit-self, which is the source of true peace.

A comment on this Beatitude preserved in ancient Church literature, apparently from the great Origenes, provides some further light,

> The Peace-makers illumine other human beings, for they are active in accordance with their capacity, in the manner of the 'sons of God'. This work being in fact, for these other human beings, reconciliation with all that the Christ accomplished {*through the Mystery of Golgotha*}.[84]
> (transl. the author)

The implication here is that Origenes is aware that an initiate who has developed the Spirit-self – the source of actual inner peace – subtly assists other people to spiritualize their own soul, and to live in harmony with the Christ-light permeating the planet. Or, in the theological terms of Origenes, these Peace-makers bring reconciliation of human beings to Christ.

Beatitude 8: (contemplating the Life-spirit)
"Blessed are those who are persecuted for righteousness' sake; for in their self they shall find the Kingdom of the Heavens."

It is clear from anthroposophical knowledge, that an initiate who has developed the Life-spirit possesses immense creative powers. Such a person is tending towards becoming a 'co-creator' to the gods, for their presence and, of course, their actions, can literally impact the environment for the better. The selfless raying-out of divine energies nurtures and heals the life-forces maintaining the natural world, and assists creative people to have their intuitive, artistic or therapeutic insights. The implication of this Beatitude is that such

---

[83] The 'John' who wrote this Gospel was Lazaros-John; see my *Rudolf Steiner on Leonardo's Last Supper* for more about this.
[84] Klostermann, (ref. 9) in the Catenae, p. 50.

advanced people are directly exposed to hostility from malignant spiritual powers.

Also, as we noted earlier, a cycle of seven has been completed with the eighth Beatitude; what has been sought for in the first phase, is now attained in the eighth. In the first Beatitude, the human being is one who is seeking spirituality, or the Spiritual-self; whereas in the eighth Beatitude, the Life-spirit has developed. It is an example of the Alpha and Omega dynamic. We need to note that the 1st and the 8th Beatitudes have the same phrase in them:

"for of their self is the Kingdom of the Heavens."

Or, in Rudolf Steiner's translation,

"for in their self they shall find the Kingdom of the Heavens."

Although there is no difference in the Greek text to show this, the meaning in the first Beatitude is different to that of the 8th Beatitude. In the first Beatitude, that message is that the spiritual seeker has a connection with the spiritual worlds; they are being inspired from their Higher-self. Whereas in the 8th Beatitude the message is, that the now initiated, sanctified human being has achieved the transformation of their personality or earthly-ego, into the Higher-self. (See his brief comments again, in Chapter Six, (p.91).

Beatitude 9: (contemplating the Spirit-human)
  "Blessed are you, when people revile you and persecute you, for my sake".

Nothing else can really be added to the brief commentaries from Rudolf Steiner about this Beatitude, as it refers to a remote future time, and we have no knowledge as to what the Earth and humanity shall be experiencing in this future age, the timing of which is not specified.

Final thoughts:

The last words about the Beatitudes, in Matthew's Gospel (5: 12), which summarize their significance, proclaim that the spiritualized souls may rejoice. But this brings us again to the passage in St. Luke's Gospel (chapter 6:23) where scholars incorrectly see a close similarity to two or three of the Beatitudes. St. Luke records the words, "Rejoice in that day...."

St. Matthew also has at the end of the nine Beatitudes, "rejoice and....". But the context of St. Luke's words is, as we noted earlier, that they were given 'on the plain', and not 'on the mountain'. So with the scene in Luke's Gospel, Christ is referring to personal challenges for the general populace, for the crowds who were following him.

Hence, in saying 'rejoice' to these people, Christ was saying, (as his Aramaic words are translated into Greek by the Gospel writer) through the use of a particular form of a Greek verb, "*joy shall be conferred upon you, as a **once-off** experience*".[85] In fact, the entire passage in Luke's Gospel is about human beings in earthly life,

> Lk 6:22 Blessed are you when men hate you, when they exclude you and insult you and reject your name as evil, because of the Son of Man.
> Lk 6:23 **Rejoice in that day** and leap for joy, because great is your reward in heaven. For that is how their fathers treated the prophets.
> Lk 6:24 But woe to you who are rich, for you have already received your comfort.

Whereas in Matthew's Gospel, Christ 'from the mountain top', proclaims something quite different, in a much more exalted context:

> Mt 5:12 **Be rejoicing and be over-joyed,** because great is your reward in Heaven, for in the same way they persecuted the prophets who were before you.

Here Christ uses a word which is also normally translated as 'rejoice', but which actually means 'an **on-going** joy is yours, for you yourself have attained it', (and not a one-off joy conferred upon you).[86] In addition, to emphasize the glorious state of initiated souls, we need to notice that Christ says also, 'be over-joyed', (hagalliaoe - ἀγαλλιάω). Despite this strong meaning of the rare verb used here, to be 'over-joyed' or 'rejoice exceedingly', it is translated in many versions simply as 'be glad'. Yet this verb was actually created by Christian writers in the first century, for such occasions, and actually means 'to be over-joyed', or to rejoice exceedingly, or to exult.

So, we can once again see the difference between the passage from Luke's Gospel, recording an incident involving

---

[85] This form is known as 'a passive aorist', (xaraete - χάρητε).
[86] Technically the verb is in the 'present active imperative' form (χαίρητε).

teaching a large crowd, and that of Matthew's Gospel, where an initiatory teaching is revealed in secret, to the Disciples. This is what the cosmic Christ experienced, as this great Being surveyed the potential opportunity for humanity to evolve towards the spirit, into far future time-cycles, once the Mystery of Golgotha had taken place. For from this sacrifice the planet shall be permeated with treasuries of divine light, from which the human spirit can grow and blossom – if people so will.

The significance of the Beatitudes is profoundly summed up in these words by Rudolf Steiner:

> In these wonderful sentences, which refer to the nine members of human nature, it is shown how the "I" forms itself with regard to the various members of human nature, when it becomes a 'Christ-I', and how this {*higher*} "I" blesses these aspects of the human being. In these sentences, which follow the Temptation scene, is brought to expression in a magnificent way, in a majestic way, in the Gospel of Matthew, how the Christ-power exerts its influence on the nine members of the human being.
>
> He shows how this occurs, first in the contemporary times, and then how this power shall exert its efficacy in the near future, wherein those people shall be called 'children of God', into whom the Spirit-self is already shining its radiance. But only a few of such people exist, people who have received the Grace {*spiritual radiance from the Christ*} that has made this possible.
>
> Precisely this is the wonderful aspect to these Beatitudes: the words spoken specifically about the first of the nine members, which are already there, {*and being transformed*}; and then with the later Beatitudes the focus goes out into the indeterminate far future, regarding the last of the nine members {*which still have to be brought into birth*}.[87]

---

[87] From Source 'E', GA 123, *The Gospel of Matthew*, lecture 9th Sept. 1910.

Conclusion

We have studied all of the commentaries on the Beatitudes which Rudolf Steiner provided, and in this work, explored these sayings from the original Greek text of the Gospel. In considering the ancient Greek, we have encountered perspectives which arise as a result of the new method of assessing Gospel texts which I have developed.

In our exploration of the Beatitudes this text assessment method (or 'critical path') has often confirmed the validity of Rudolf Steiner's understanding of the Beatitudes. This work has been done with acknowledgement of theological understanding of these sayings, and with the inclusion of some rare commentaries, surviving from the great Origenes.

The outcome of this is that we became aware that the Beatitudes have a meaning, previously unknown, which interweaves a large, cosmic view of creation with the potential for higher development of human beings, in future Ages.

The Beatitudes are understood as guidance from the cosmic Christ, serving as a series of helpful sign-posts along the great journey that the human life-wave has embarked on. Taking notice of these sign-posts empowers us in our own quest for a true, higher Self, and to thereby assist our fellow human beings on their pathway.

Appendix 1

The astral body as separate from the sentient-soul

It is difficult to have a clear understanding of this point. The soul, also called the astral body, or soul-body, is understood in anthroposophy to consist of feelings, thinking and will. So how can the soul-body be a different thing to the feelings or 'sentient-soul'? Rudolf Steiner teaches that these are separate, yet in the perceiving by the clairvoyant, these two appear to be almost the same thing; for example,

> "The sentient-soul is inwardly united with the astral body, **as if embedded in it.**"[88]

> Now in the clairvoyant perceiving, the soul-body and the sentient-soul **can not be perceived as separate** entities. The sentient-soul is placed inside the soul-body, like a sword in its sheath. These two are called the astral body.[89]

It is the following words in the same lecture which provide a starting point of clarity about these two aspects of our nature,

> ....then we come to what actually lives in the human being; namely **the soul can perceive (register) a sentient experience**; and with this, we **rise up from the soul-body to the sentient-soul**, the lowest member of the soul.[90]

In other words, it is the presence of a consciousness which registers sensory impressions and such basic feelings as pleasure and pain, which **is** the sentient-soul. The following words clarify this further,

> ...in that moment, where we begin to inwardly experience {our environment or our inner responses}, **there** begins what we call the sentient-soul, as distinct from what is the sentient-body {or *'astral body'*}...there where inner experiencing commences, there begins the sentient-soul, as distinct from the astral body.[91]

---

[88] GA 101, lecture, 27th Dec. 1907, p. 210.
[89] GA 53, lecture, 13th Oct. 1904, p.56.
[90] ibid.
[91] GA 58, lecture, 11th Nov. 1909, p. 57.

The last piece of the puzzle is this: that Rudolf Steiner, when speaking in a very precise manner, defines the astral body or soul-body, as the aura of astral energies which, in a remote aeon, descended from the hosts of divine-spiritual beings, and enveloped our primordial physical-etheric body. As a result, the primitive human being began to register, and to be aware of, environmental influences and inner sensations, such as fear, pleasure, and pain. Then the mere auric glow of astral energy developed an inner life: the sentient-soul.

The sentient-soul is composed of our emotional nature (desires, fears, yearnings and so on) and our sentient capacities, (awareness of, and response to, the environment): to its cold and warmth, etc. So Rudolf Steiner is defining the sentient-soul as a tangible individuated consciousness weaving through this aura of astral energies – in the form of emotions and responses to environmental conditions. In his words,

> Here we have to be as sharply differentiating as when sorting out two hairs from each other: that which, from outside, is magically conjured up in front of us {*as a field of astral energies by the gods in remote ages*}, **this** is what has brought about the soul-body (astral-body); but that which we inwardly experience, **that** is the point of origin of the sentient-soul.[92]

This point becomes clearer once we read the description of how the gods brought the human being into existence in his book, *An Outline of Esoteric Science.*

---

[92] GA119, lecture, 22nd Mar. 1910 p. 71.

Appendix 2

The Essenes and the first Beatitude

The Dead Sea Scrolls are 2,000 year old texts found at Qumran in Palestine, in the mid-twentieth century, which are a testimony to the beliefs and religious life of the Essenes, who were one of several religious groups prominent in the Jewish community. In one of these scrolls, there is a hymn which, as so often in these scrolls, refers to the yearning of the Essenes for a time when the Messiah appears, and when evil is overcome. It has such phrases as,

> He has called those who are tottering, to {*achieve*} wondrous exploits, and had gathered the {*antagonistic*} nations for destruction, with no remnants ...to those with knocking knees, he gives strength to stand upright...

But the next sentence in this hymn appears to echo a key phrase in the first Beatitude. It is usually translated as,

> "Among the poor in spirit is power (or 'authority') over a hard heart."[93]

But the Hebrew grammar here also allows this sentence to be translated as,

> "**In** the poor in spirit is power (or authority) over a hard heart."[94]

And this is indeed similar to the Beatitude. The phrase 'a hard heart' probably means, *those other ones who have* a hardened heart. In any event, how does this text compare to the first Beatitude? Although this Beatitude is about those who are 'beggars for the spirit', and not 'poor in spirit', there is of course, a similarity between the two words, and the two ideas. Beggars are actively seeking to relieve their poverty, whereas 'the poor' is a more passive term.

So the possibility does exist that the Essenes were aware of the truth that underlies the first Beatitude; the loss of the age-old spiritual awareness. However, Rudolf Steiner emphasizes that the Essenes' primary interest in adopting a spiritual way of life, was to do with an inner purification, to fit themselves

---

[93] *The War Rule* 1QM 14:5-6.

[94] The phrase in the scrolls is: בעניי רוה, and the small preposition used by the Essenes here (*Beth,* ב) in this sentence, can mean 'in', or 'among'.

to have a closeness with the Messiah, the Christ-impulse, derived from the teachings of their great leader, Jesus ben Pandira. But perhaps the Essenes thought of themselves as inwardly being no longer naturally spiritually perceptive, and this became a factor in their dedication to a spiritual way of life.

If this is the case, then this verse here could be saying that, we Essenes acknowledge the lack of a spiritual awareness in our souls, and we are seeking to remedy this, and indeed there is now a spiritual force developing in the soul.

The question has to remain unanswered, but there is an intriguing similarity to the first Beatitude. In any event, these words suggest that the Essenes felt they were empowered over a cold heart-quality in their own personality, (or, over those people who are inwardly cold). And therefore, in harmony with their future expectations, these Essenes formed their core belief, namely that they shall triumph over evil.

Appendix 3

Last section of the 1905 lecture

Let us bring to mind what in an earlier lecture, I called the "northern cultural stream", or rather the cultural stream that {*over the course of the Post-Atlantean Ages*} goes from East to West: the {*primal*} Indian-Persian-Germanic stream. On the other hand, we have the other stream which encompasses the Chaldean-Assyrian-Babylonian-Egyptian civilizations. We need to differentiate between these two streams. To the esotericist, these are in contrast to the one which comes from Spain and which gave the last impulse to the Middle Ages and which must be replaced by the (Sanskrit) Indian-Persian-Germanic stream.

> Note:
> We are reminded again that the notes taken of the lecturer's words are somewhat brief. The designation here of earlier cultural streams differs slightly from his usual use of names. The actual cultural Ages of the Post-Atlantean Age are, (so far): the ancient Indian, ancient Persian, Egyptian-Mesopotamian, Greco-Latin, and our own Germanic/Anglo-American Age. The phrase, "the Chaldean-Assyrian-Babylonian-Egyptian stream" clearly refers to the Third Post-Atlantean cultures, also known as the Egyptian-Mesopotamian Age. However the "Indian-Persian-Germanic stream" is a more unusual, abbreviated designation; it would normally be, the "Indian-Persian-Germanic/Anglo-American stream".

> But in a lecture about the scenes of the Mysteries painted on the small Cupola of the Goetheanum, given as it was being built, Rudolf Steiner described the initiation principle of the *Germanic(-Anglo-American) Age* (*i.e., Anthroposophy*) as factoring in that kind of spiritual duality which was a main feature of the ancient Persian culture: the battle between Light and Darkness. The ancient Persians had this polarity of light and darkness as a prominent feature of their religion, as distinct from a triune god, or an em-bracing Oneness.

So, the *"Persian-Germanic stream"* refers to the dualistic worldview with regard to spiritual realities, held in common by the old Zarathustrian religion and the modern western world. Although, there is a difference between the duality of the ancient primal Persian and the new anthroposophical spiritual path. As he commented in his lecture, in today's world, the spiritual seeker "must seek a condition of balance between Lucifer and Ahriman".[95] (Whereas in old Persia it was a struggle between Ahriman and the sun-god.)

In contrast to the above stream, the cultural-religious impulse "which comes from Spain and which gave the last impulse to the Middle Ages" appears to refer to the Ottoman Empire.

(Lecture continues)
The sixth cultural epoch shall be entirely governed {*in terms of spiritual aspirations*} by this 'northern cultural stream' {*the central European spirituality*}.

> Note:
> For the next cultural epoch to be 'governed', i.e., sustained and inspired, by the spirituality of the central European world of our Age, appears to mean that the spiritual wisdom and integrity developed in this Age, shall underlie the next Age. But only after this spiritual wisdom has been metamorphosed and strengthened in the soul. It can then manifest in a new way, once people are incarnated in the next Age, which commences in the 36th century.

(Lecture continues)
But we human beings can only achieve that which must be achieved, if we {*really*} are self-aware beings. That is to say, if we actually recognize what needs to be achieved. However the theosophists(-*anthroposophists*) are **not**[96] the least of those

---

[95] Lecture, 25th Jan. 1920 (not yet in the Complete Works; published as a separate booklet.)
[96] A major difference occurs here in the Archive book: the word "not" is omitted, reversing the meaning of the sentence, which is saying that actually the theosophists (-anthroposophists) have a major role ("are **not** among the least") in explaining what is to come about, what we need to meet the future

121

who declare what is to take place; {*i.e., the wisdom of anthroposophy will actually be a major force preparing for this future spirituality*}. Such future situations shall certainly arise, but {*for this to actually happen in the next Age*} people need to act now, so as to enable this future to come about.

For this purpose we should steep ourselves in that which world history has given us as our task. We need to perceive what is in decline, and what is now having its dawn. The tasks of the gods have to be achieved on this Earth **through human beings**. We have to take hold of what is contained within the rising {*spiritual-*}sun. {*This refers to so-called Second Coming of Jesus, more accurately understood in anthroposophy as the Etheric Reappearing of Jesus; and means the enlightening and healing influence raying out from Jesus Christ, from within the Earth's etheric aura.*} Karma is not a fatalistic law; karma is a law of nature. But just as little as water can result from combining oxygen and hydrogen, if the chemist does not mix them together, so also karma cannot bring forth something new, if the human being does not act. We have to recognize what this means: to exert, in a Christian sense, an influence on the future.

The vessel of the lower, personal self has been handed on to us from {*the result of our evolving during*} past Ages. This vessel has played an important role in the long materialistic Age, which in fact, is now over. The higher aspect of the human being shall raise itself up out of the elements and reveal itself in its glory.

People don't consider the history of our times deeply enough. Materialism has reached its furthest point; it has reached an extreme level. Consider just some small symptoms that are decisive for those who can gaze into their significance. Some hours before this lecture, I read in the newspaper, about a Minister who had resigned from his position. I read there a sentence in the leading article, from the "New Independent Press", which expressed a deeply ironical fact about our entire tines.

If it is possible for habitual ways of thinking to so extensively master a person, that he dares to write such a sentence, then

---

as best we can. Without the 'not', it means the theosophists **have the least to offer** when considering what we need to understand, to meet the future. Since these words refer to Rudolf Steiner above all, this official version appears to be in error.

the inner nature of such a person is empty. The sentence is: "*What I have emphasized of the normal human being, already when he was still Minister, when no-one could know how it was linked to the fall of his career, is this: the complete earnestness of his goals.*" {*The implication of these words is that*} it is actually possible, that one of the senior statesmen can have goals which are **not** earnest, not genuine ! So, {*this sentence reveals that*} the time has arrived in which a man whom people call "great' means simply one who has genuine goals.

Materialism had to be in existence. It has given us our external cultural achievements; we don't want to complain and raise an outcry against it. We want to acknowledge that our way of thinking, directed to the sensory world, has brought forth our industries and technology. But now the time for a new ascent is here. The human being must now go from the usual, personal, self up to the Higher-self, in the meaning of the Sermon on the Mount. The human being now has to understand the connection between lower and the higher; {*and thus bring about the nurturing and emergence of the Higher-self from within the earthly self, by conscious effort*}.

The human being has to move beyond the {*kind of*} spiritual reality which has ruled over the first five Post-Atlantean Ages. {*Furthermore*}, there is also much {*existing*} in the vessel {*of the human soul*} which is impersonal: this has come about in an impersonal {*unthinking*} way, as a natural process. {*That is, attitudes and habitual ways of feeling and thinking have been absorbed from the cultural environment, without being assessed beforehand.*}

For the theosophist(-*anthroposophist*) it is completely foreign to regard these aspects of human nature in any other way than objectively. No personality is to be disparaged. Therefore, what I have presented to you here is also meant in an objective sense, and is to be understood merely as a symbol of a materialism, which has already overcome itself. Two people have recently died within a short space of time from each other. {*These were members of the super-rich Rothschild dynasty.*}

It would no longer be possible today for that symbol of the international House of Rothschild - the symbol of the five arrows - which was so significant, to again reach such mighty power. This five-fold arrow symbol signified that in various parts of Europe, for some considerable time, extending into the latter part of the 19th century, this international banking concern exerted an effect which was a united reality; it worked as one unified impulse.

In this impulse there was active the entirely personal {*earthly*} self; and in its last phase, it exerted more impact than anyone can ever sense, who understands history only from the outside. Such people do not sense how this enterprise has come into being from the spirit of materialism; this materialism which has burdened our lands, to the extent that the history of our nation can no longer be understood without bearing in mind this materialistic mindset {*and its far-reaching effects*}.

End of lecture

Note:
It appears that the very end of the lecture was not recorded in this manuscript. It basically finished with references to the inherently wrong nature of a concentration of wealth in a relatively small number of people, who use their wealth for their own interests. Although Rudolf Steiner mentions only one such dynasty, there were and are a number of other family dynasties or small groups not related to each other.

It appears that, in doing this, Rudolf Steiner was urging the audience to awaken to the harmful nature of the way that society is structured. In anthroposophy, society is seen as having three spheres or facets to it – the Commercial sphere, the sphere of legislation or Rights, and the Cultural sphere. These are currently interrelated in a really unwholesome way; in particular, the Commercial sphere dominates the other two sectors of society, in a disastrous way.

If there is to be a more harmonious world, with the cultural-spiritual aspects of society able to contribute in the best way, thus allowing, amongst other impulses, for inspiration from the Christ-impulse to inspire humanity, and nourish the potential for spirituality in the soul, then the egoistical, anti-social quest for excessive wealth and the interrelated ruinous demands on the Earth's resources, has to stop.

In fact, the keynote role of the Commercial sphere, the sector of society that generates wealth, is meant to be Fraternity. That is, a fraternal spirit should underlie the distribution of goods and services, to ensure that the non-commercial sphere – the educational needs, artistic gifts, medical research, and spiritual nurture, etc, are allowed to flourish, without having to identify a commercial viability. The good-will and altruism that would enable this to happen, is seen as a response to the influences raying forth the new phase of interaction between humanity and the Christ-impulse.

Appendix 4

"You are gods"

There is a remarkable passage in the Gospel of John (10:34), where Jesus, speaking to a crowd, reminds his listeners, that Scripture declares that they are gods,

> *Jesus answered them, "Is it not written in your Law, 'I {Jahve} have said, you {human beings} are gods {Elohim}' "?*

This text is a quote from Psalm 82:6, where the Hebrew term used in the Psalm for 'gods' is actually 'Elohim'. These beings are the sun-spirits or 'Spirits of Form' or Powers as St. Paul calls them. So, as the higher "I" develops (the Spirit-self and Life-spirit), the advanced Christian initiate shall indeed start to "spiritually perceive a divine being-ness" in their now re-born "I". For it is from the great sun-spirits, especially the cosmic Christ, that the Spirit-self derives.

Appendix 5

The First Beatitude and the power of Christ over the physical body (Gospel of St. John, chapter17; 1-2)

We saw earlier how Rudolf Steiner explains that the first Beatitude is about the influence from Christ that enables people to seek spirituality, despite the effect of the physical body on consciousness.

At the beginning of the 17th chapter of the Gospel of St. John, there is a passage which indicates that Christ is specifically empowered to exert an influence on human beings, considered as souls within their physical flesh body. However this indication is only becomes apparent after some engagement with the Greek text. In the NIV translation it is,

> **17:1 Father, the hour has arrived: glorify your Son, that your Son may glorify you.**
> **(2) For you granted him authority over all people, so that he might give eternal life to all those you have given him.**[1]

Firstly we need to note, that these sentences are about profound themes, and are presented in especially complex grammar; so the meaning is not easily seen. And actually as part of the grammatical complexities here, the second half of verse 2 appears to be saying, if translators were to use the Greek directly as it is written:

*so that **all** **that** which Thou hast given to him, he may give to them* (*people*) *...*

But scholars conclude such a translation has to be wrong, because it cannot mean, all which Christ received from God is to be given on to people. That is, one cannot regard God as giving a gift to Christ, and that Christ then gives the same attribute to us.

So scholars agree that it has to be saying,

---

[1] The Greek text is: πάτερ, ἐλήλυθεν ἡ ὥρα· δόξασον σου τὸν υἱόν, ἵνα ὁ υἱὸς δοξάσῃ σέ, καθὼς ἔδωκας αὐτῷ ἐξουσίαν πάσης σαρκός, ἵνα πᾶν ὃ δέδωκας αὐτῷ δώσῃ αὐτοῖς ζωὴν αἰώνιον.

"so that Christ might give eternal life (*aeonic consciousness*) **to
all** *those* **whom You have given him."**

With this solution, "all" here (pan - πᾶν) is understood to mean '**all
people**', not **all the gift** given by God – but even so, for a reason
difficult to grasp, 'all' is put in the neutral gender, which the
Greek never would do (the gender for 'people' is masculine).

Now, with this part made clearer, we can move back to the earlier
part of verse 2, to try to understand more clearly the connection
of the First Beatitude to the passage. The earlier part of the
sentence is, (and I am omitting here other complex problems in
the grammar of the Greek):

 "*for you granted him authority over all people*",

Now, although this makes sense as it is, the phrase here, "all
people" (pasaes   sarkos - **πάσης σαρκός**), actually means in the
Greek, 'all corporeal earthly humanity', that is people considered
as beings living their physical bodies. So it is better translated as,
"for You gave to him power over all flesh". This is because the
Greek for term, "all flesh" is what is called a 'Hebraism', i.e., a
rendering into Greek of a Hebrew expression, common in the Old
Testament; this expression refers to human beings in the physical
body, (the same usage occurs in chap. 6;39).

It is of course, the challenge to try to understand why a phrase is
used here which focuses on the corporeal, physical aspect of
human beings, since we would expect such a high Gospel text to
refer to us as 'souls'. The solution to this enigma is found in the
light of Rudolf Steiner's commentary on the First Beatitude.

We are being told in the Gospel passage that Christ has been given
spiritual power to help human beings, but specifically **as people
living in their physical, flesh bodies.** So this is linked to the
esoteric message of the First Beatitude: that Christ has power to
spiritually assist the consciousness of people living in their
physical, flesh bodies. This interpretation is in harmony with the
Greek text, and implies what the First Beatitude indicates that,
despite the impact of the physical body on human consciousness,
Christ has the power – if the individual person so wills – to help
consciousness to transcend the physical, material world.

The underlying theme in this solemn and majestic section of the Gospel, is the imminent Crucifixion of Jesus, and therefore the events of Golgotha. So it is deeply significant that here the physical body and its effect on our consciousness is linked to the purpose of the coming of Christ to the Earth. So the verse is now:

"so that Christ might give eternal life (aeonic consciousness) to all those whom You have given him, for You gave to him power over all flesh."

INDEX

3101 BC, 47
Apollo, 99
Archangel Vidar, 95
astral realm, 76
Atma, 16, 63
become the kingdoms of
    Heaven, 28, 94
blessed, 14
Broadus, 37
Bultmann, 3
children of God, 114
clairvoyant capacity, 11, 27
Clement of Alexandria, 9
compassionate, 46
cosmic Christ, 4,5 94, 100
Cosmos Spirit, 91
counter-image, 77
currents of spiritual
    energies, 99
dative case, 24
divinely-enfilled, 47
ecstatic, 36, 100
eleeoe, 45, 104
Elohim, 4, 96
eradicate illnesses, 87
eye, 50, 54, 89
French Morality, 70
fury, 40, 84
gentleness, 84
Gospel of St. Thomas, 83
great future power, 90
Hagner, 33
Harnack, 3
healing powers, 100
Holy Spirit, 35
human I shines forth, 46
human quality, 103
in reverse, 75
In such a time, 70
in the midst of you, 82
inherit, 39
Initiatory Critical Analysis,
    3
intellectual-soul, 46, 49
kaleisthai, 55

Kali Yuga, 20, 47
kingdom of God, 81
Liberal Theology, 71
Life-Spirit, 61
Light on the Path, 38
Logos, 62
malignant elemental
    energies, 98
Manas, 57
Mars forces, 41, 85
materialism, 92
Matthew, 10, 11, 13, 18, 20,
    25, 32, 37, 53, 59, 84,
    112, 113
meek, 37
merciful, 106
mercy, 45, 104
Mights, 102
mirror-image, 75, 90
Mitleid, 45
Moon Aeon, 40, 102
mountain, 11, 12, 13, 14,
    20, 21, 64, 72, 73, 92,
    112, 113
Muses, 99
Origenes, 4, 9, 10, 50, 53,
    54, 84, 97, 110, 115
Paraclete, 35
peace-maker, 9, 55, 56,
    65,11
Plato, 83
Portia, 104
Psalm 37, v.11, 37
replica of the physical
    body, 96
rhythmical, 66
righteousness, 42, 44, 87
satiation, 87
seated himself, 13
sentient-soul, 43
Septuagint, 33
Shakespeare, 104
Sphinx, 102
Spirit-self, 56, 57, 95
spirituality, 42, 102

spiritual-soul, 51
St. Luke, 7, 10, 14, 81, 112
Tertullian, 24
The 'nine-fold' human being, 15
The Hymn to Apollo, 99
these people **were realms**, 28

Ulrich Lux, 25
Virgin Birth, 95
von Goethe, 78
white lily-bud, 95
Wilhelm Meister, 78
yearning for the Spirit, 79

Other books by this Author

Living a Spiritual Year: seasonal festivals in both hemispheres	1992
(new, expanded edition, 2016)	
The Way to the Sacred	2003
The Foundation Stone Meditation: a new commentary	2005
Dramatic Anthroposophy: Identification and contextualization of primary features of Rudolf Steiner's anthroposophy. (PhD thesis)	2005
Two Gems from Rudolf Steiner	2014
The Hellenistic Mysteries & Christianity	2014
Rudolf Steiner Handbook	2014
Horoscope Handbook – a Rudolf Steiner Approach	2015
The Meaning of the Goetheanum Windows	2016
Rudolf Steiner's Esoteric Christianity in the Grail painting by Anna May	2017
The Vidar Flame Column – its meaning from Rudolf Steiner	2017

See also as Damien Pryor:

The nature & origin of the Tropical Zodiac	2011
Stonehenge	2011
The Externsteine	2011
Lalibela	2011
The Great Pyramid & the Sphinx	2011

Website: www.rudolfsteinerstudies.com

This site has information on all of these books, as well as free downloads of various essays, and a link to the author's ARTPRINTS page, which offers esoteric diagrams and great classical works of art which are relevant to the understanding of anthroposophy.

There is also a Donate page.

www.ingramcontent.com/pod-product-compliance
Lightning Source LLC
Chambersburg PA
CBHW071812090426
42737CB00012B/2052